"*The Play Cycle in Practice* is a very welcome resource for the children's services sector. The discussion about the features of children at play and playing is insightful. The reflective questions throughout help adults to understand the connections with children and their role in play. Understanding the Play Cycle helps adults to be effective in their work with children. Children's play is predominantly a child-focused initiative. However, organisations in society have deemed that adults have a responsibility to be part of this process. The discussion and examples about the Play Cycle are predominantly gathered from the United Kingdom. Nonetheless, each of the chapters contains elements that are highly relevant to international communities. Understanding the Play Cycle means that adults can understand more deeply children's perspectives and behaviours.

This book is relevant to a wide range of disciplines including educators, teachers, occupational therapists, play therapists, and social workers who work with children and young people. The ideas about the Play Cycle are applicable in a diverse range of settings including early childhood centres, adventure playgrounds, schools kindergartens, and hospital play therapy centres just to name a few. It is an essential resource for those who are interested in children and young people's play."

*Dr Jennifer Cartmel,*
*Associate Professor, Griffith University, Australia*

"This book provides a practical and insightful view of the Play Cycle and its relevance today for anyone working with children. The importance of play is central to the chapters, outlining how the Play Cycle can be implemented and the significance of this for developing reflective professionals. The vignettes and quotes from those working with the Play Cycle provide relevant and real-life examples from practice. Navigating the different situations and systems where the Play Cycle is relevant can be complex. The reflective questions in each chapter support self-reflection and develop confidence for those familiar with or new to the Play Cycle."

*Dr Natalie Canning,*
*The Open University, UK*

# THE PLAY CYCLE IN PRACTICE

This book explores how the Play Cycle can help practitioners to observe and understand children's play and support their interactions with children. It explains the six elements of the Play Cycle – pre cue, play cue, play return, play frame, flow, and annihilation – and shows how practitioners can use this to guide their interventions.

Building on the author's research and including an updated and revised theory of the Play Cycle, the book applies the Play Cycle to key aspects of provision alongside examples from a wide range of settings. Chapters cover:

- The indoor and outdoor environment and resources
- Child-led and non-directive play including risk
- The adult role, play maintenance and interventions
- The Play Cycle and Play Cycle Observation Method
- The Play Cycle in Policy and Practice

Including vignettes and reflective questions, this text brings the theory and application of the Play Cycle fully up-to-date and is essential reading for practitioners and those studying play-related courses, for example, playwork, childcare, and early years education.

**Pete King** is Senior Lecturer at Swansea University and the Programme Director for the MA in Developmental and Therapeutic Play. He is co-author of *The Play Cycle: Theory, Research and Application*, and his research has been published both nationally and internationally in academic journals. Pete has been involved in children's play since 1996 and this book is a combination of nearly 30 years professional practice, teaching, and research.

# THE PLAY CYCLE IN PRACTICE

Supporting, Observing, and Reflecting on Children's Play

Pete King

LONDON AND NEW YORK

Designed cover image: Lisa Dynan

First edition published 2026
by Routledge
4 Park Square, Milton Park, Abingdon, Oxon, OX14 4RN

and by Routledge
605 Third Avenue, New York, NY 10158

*Routledge is an imprint of the Taylor & Francis Group, an informa business*

© 2026 Pete King

The right of Pete King to be identified as author of this work has been asserted in accordance with sections 77 and 78 of the Copyright, Designs and Patents Act 1988.

All rights reserved. No part of this book may be reprinted or reproduced or utilised in any form or by any electronic, mechanical, or other means, now known or hereafter invented, including photocopying and recording, or in any information storage or retrieval system, without permission in writing from the publishers.

*Trademark notice*: Product or corporate names may be trademarks or registered trademarks, and are used only for identification and explanation without intent to infringe.

*British Library Cataloguing-in-Publication Data*
A catalogue record for this book is available from the British Library

ISBN: 978-1-032-97679-2 (hbk)
ISBN: 978-1-032-97677-8 (pbk)
ISBN: 978-1-003-59481-9 (ebk)

DOI: 10.4324/9781003594819

Typeset in Interstate
by KnowledgeWorks Global Ltd.

**DEDICATION**

This book is dedicated to the late Gordon Sturrock, the late Professor Perry Else, and the late Bob Hughes.

# CONTENTS

*List of figures and tables* — xii
*Foreword by Dr Shelly Newstead and Kathy Brodie* — xiii
*Acknowledgments* — xvi
*Glossary* — xvii

**Introduction: The Play Cycle: how it all began** — 1
*Introduction* 1
*A personal reflection on the Play Cycle* 1
*Defining play* 2
*The process of play* 4
*The different types of play environments* 4
*The structure of the book* 6
*Conclusion* 7

1 **The Play Cycle revised and updated** — 8
*Introduction* 8
*Where it all began* 8
*Revising and updating the Play Cycle* 9
*Developing the theory behind the Play Cycle* 10
*The adult role in the Play Cycle* 11
*A summary of the Play Cycle* 12
*Examples of the Play Cycle being used in practice* 12
*Observing and recording the Play Cycle* 13
*Conclusion* 14

2 **The Play Cycle and the play environment** — 15
*Introduction* 15
*The play environment or the 'Ludic ecology'* 15
*The Play Cycle and the Functional Cycle* 16
*The play environment and affordances* 17
*The indoor and outdoor play environment, play types, and affordances* 18
*Loose parts* 20
*Types of play* 23
*Conclusion* 25

x Contents

## 3 The Play Cycle and child-led play 26
*Introduction* 26
*The Right to Play and the United Nations Convention on the Rights of the Child* 26
*Defining child-centred, child-directed, child-initiated, and child-led* 27
*The Play Cycle and child-led play* 28
*The Play Cycle and non-directive play* 30
*The Play Cycle and risk in play* 32
*Conclusion* 34

## 4 The Play Cycle and the role of the adult 35
*Introduction* 35
*How adults support the process of play* 35
*The Play Cycle: Play maintenance, simple involvement, medial intervention, and complex intervention* 36
*Play maintenance* 36
*The Play Cycle and AIS* 39
*The adult role in the Play Cycle and PBL* 40
*Reflective practice* 43
*Reflection-in-action and reflection-on-action* 44
*The Play Cycle and reflective practice* 45
*Conclusion* 47

## 5 The Play Cycle Observation Method (PCOM) 48
*Introduction* 48
*The PCOM resources* 48
*The PCOM application* 49
*Example of a PCOM observation using a recorded video of children playing* 52
*Transferring the information to the PCOM Record Sheet Table* 54
*The role of the adult in the PCOM* 56
*The PCOM analysis* 57
*Play cue issued* 57
*Play return* 58
*Time* 59
*Play cues initiated in established Play Cycles* 59
*Interpreting the data* 60
*Undertaking the PCOM in real-time* 62
*The PCOM and other play observational tools* 63
*Conclusion* 63

## 6 The Play Cycle in policy and practice 65
*Introduction* 65
*Government play policies and strategies and the UNCRC* 65
*The Children Act and regulation and inspection of childcare settings* 68
*The Play Cycle and the NMS* 70
*The Play Cycle and the NOS* 72
*The Play Cycle – Performance Criteria/Learning Outcomes and Knowledge, Skills, and Understanding/Aims* 75
*Higher education and practitioner status* 75
*Conclusion* 78

**Conclusion: A brief recap of the Play Cycle and potential
challenges for professional practice** 80
*Introduction* 80
*A brief recap* 80
*The potential challenges in applying the Play Cycle in professional practice* 82
*Play perceived in policy and legislation* 82
*Play perceived in professional qualifications* 83
*Context of play in professional practice* 83
*Individual perceptions of play* 84
*Conclusion – A final thought* 84

*Appendix* 86
*References* 89
*Index* 101

# LIST OF FIGURES AND TABLES

## Figures

| | | |
|---|---|---|
| Figure 1.1 | An updated version of the Play Cycle | 12 |
| Figure 4.1 | The Play Cycle and the Adult Intervention Style | 40 |
| Figure 4.2 | Types of play and adult role in PBL (based on Bergen, 1988; Pyle & Danniels, 2017) (Source King, 2025). | 41 |
| Figure 4.3 | Level of intervention and adult role in PBL (Source King, 2025) | 42 |
| Figure 5.1 | The Play Cycle Observation Method (PCOM) Record Sheet | 49 |
| Figure 5.2 | PCOM Record Sheet Example 1 | 53 |
| Figure 5.3 | PCOM Record Sheet Example 2 | 53 |
| Figure 5.4 | PCOM Record Sheet Example 3 | 54 |
| Figure C.1 | Key aspects of child-led, adult-led, and collaborative play with the play cycle | 81 |
| Figure C.2 | The Play Cycle and potential areas of challenge | 82 |
| Figure A.1 | Play Cycle Observation Method (PCOM) Record Sheet | 86 |

## Tables

| | | |
|---|---|---|
| Table 4.1 | Reflective guide and the Play Cycle | 45 |
| Table 5.1 | The Play Cycle Observation Method (PCOM) Record Sheet Table | 50 |
| Table 5.2 | The Play Cycle Observation Method (PCOM) Record Sheet Example 1 | 55 |
| Table 5.3 | The Play Cycle Observation Method (PCOM) Record Sheet Example 2 | 61 |
| Table 5.4 | The PCOM Frequency and Percentage Table | 62 |
| Table 6.3 | Current vocational courses | 74 |
| Table 6.4 | Key areas, keywords, and the Play Cycle | 76 |
| Table A.1 | Play Cycle Observation Method (PCOM) Record Sheet Table | 87 |
| Table A.2 | Play Cycle Observation Method (PCOM) Frequency and Percentage Table | 88 |

# FOREWORD BY DR SHELLY NEWSTEAD AND KATHY BRODIE

In 2018, I had the privilege of attending the last ever PlayEducation event. Bob Hughes and Gordon Sturrock invited key players from the playwork sector to a two-day seminar in Cambridge, with the aim of advancing the eternal 'what is playwork?' conundrum. One poignant memory from that event was Gordon telling the group that he was deeply disappointed that the Play Cycle theory wasn't being used as widely as he and his co-author, Perry Else, had hoped. As somebody who had been teaching the Play Cycle internationally and seen it shift thinking and practice in adults around the world, it made me sad to think that the authors of this seminal playwork theory had no idea of its global impact on children.

In 2017 Pete King got in touch to tell me that, as 2018 was the 20th anniversary of the publication of the Play Cycle theory, something needed to be done to mark it. I always remember this with a giggle, as I had published Gordon and Perry's Therapeutic Reader One (which included the Colorado Paper) and the forthcoming anniversary had completely passed me by. Over the last few years, Pete's ingenuity and insight has resulted in a significant body of new literature which builds on Sturrock and Else's original work. It has been a real pleasure to work on several Play Cycle projects with Pete and to incorporate some of his other research into theoretical and practical resources which are now being used internationally.

One of the Play Cycle projects I was particularly pleased to be involved in was the publication of Routledge's *The Play Cycle – Theory, Research and Application* book, which included a chapter by Gordon. Whilst the book was being written, there were numerous emails back and forwards between Pete, Gordon and myself – some practical, some whimsical, some deeply philosophical and some downright depressing. Gordon knew that his days were numbered – literally – and was bearing his illness with his customary no-nonsense approach to life (and death), still deeply engaged in wanting his words to make a difference. Sadly, the published book arrived at his home just a couple of days too late, but he knew it was on its way and had been fully involved in the process – which I suspect, for Gordon, would have been the most important thing.

*The Play Cycle in Practice: Supporting, Observing and Reflecting on Children's Play* is another testament to Pete's commitment to developing the Play Cycle theory for the benefit of adults and children anywhere and everywhere. Much of the original Play Cycle theory is obscured by its depth psychology origins, but the significance of this book is that it blends the academic and the practical in a way that will enable adults to confidently use the Play Cycle wherever they find themselves around playing children. Whilst Gordon might not have agreed with every single sentence, he certainly would have approved of this book's intentions, and I hope that Pete gets the recognition he deserves for increasing access to this important playwork theory.

**Dr Shelly Newstead**
Common Threads Playwork

Children will find opportunities to play, wherever they are – at home, at nursery, or in the after-school club. It is fundamental to their wellbeing, as well as being a Right enshrined in legislation such as the UN Convention on the Rights of the Child (UNCRC).

It's also fair to say that most practitioners and educators find children's play fascinating. I know I have watched and wondered at the motivation around the transformation of a simple cardboard box into a rocket, Santa's sleigh or a racing car – sometimes all in one game! As a reflective practitioner you may also have wondered, as I have, how to support, encourage and develop that play, without subverting or adulterating it.

The Play Cycle offers the opportunity to understand children's play in an elegant, but familiar, way. It's a fascinating and practical lens through which you can support children's play more effectively. First introduced by Gordon Sturrock and Perry Else in 1998 in the conference paper now commonly known as the 'Colorado Paper', this insightful framework will help you make sense of the complex interactions between the children's internal world and their external environment during play.

Dr Pete King, or more commonly known as 'Pete', has spent decades studying, researching and developing aspects of the Play Cycle, making it more accessible and useful for everyone working with children. His experience is obvious throughout the book but, more importantly, his style of writing brings the theory to life. In this book, Pete shows us how to recognise the whole Play Cycle, from reading children's play cues and responding appropriately, to ensuring we support rather than adulterate their play experiences.

This book arrives at a crucial time in Early Years Education. With increasing pressure on Early Years settings and schools to demonstrate outcomes and impact, the Early Years sector risks losing sight of what matters to children the most about play – the natural process of play itself. The Play Cycle is a timely and much-needed reminder that play is not just about the end product, but about the journey, the process, the experiences.

When Pete first explained the Play Cycle to me, it made so much sense. I could easily visualise the way that a play idea, or pre-cue, forms in a child's mind and how that play intention is communicated in a variety of ways through different play cues. The many ways that the play could then develop and expand, and then the all-important adult's role, which is summarised into four interventions in the Play Cycle framework. As a theory it accurately reflects the seemingly inexplicable complexities of children's play and how adults can help (or hinder!).

What makes this book particularly valuable is how Pete bridges theory and practice. Drawing on extensive research from around the world, as well as real examples and his own considerable experience, he clearly demonstrates how the Play Cycle can transform pedagogy to support children's play and learning.

*Foreword by Dr Shelly Newstead and Kathy Brodie* xv

I'm particularly delighted that the book has a whole chapter on an exploration of the adult's role in the Play Cycle. Pete explains the four levels of Adult Intervention Styles (AIS) through real-life examples and worked case-studies, clearly explaining how practitioners and educators can benefit from understanding the Play Cycle. This careful and difficult balance of appropriate interventions is at the heart of quality practice in Early Years settings. When done properly, it can be transformative for children's lives.

Another very useful inclusion in this book is the in-depth exploration of the Play Cycle Observation Method (PCOM), which provides a practical tool for observing and recording children's play. Pete explains how this structured approach will help you to:

- Document the flow of play more systematically
- Reflect on our practice more effectively
- Make informed decisions about when to intervene
- Support children's play more intentionally
- Understand how the environment supports different play types

Throughout the whole book, Pete skilfully weaves together research evidence, theoretical understanding and practical application. He shows you how the Play Cycle can be used across different types of Early Years settings – from nurseries to after-school clubs, from outdoor spaces to Playwork environments. It is this versatility and application through first-hand experience that makes the book relevant for anyone working with children in play-based contexts.

Perhaps most importantly, this book reminds us all that play is children's natural way of learning about themselves and their world. By understanding the Play Cycle and trusting in children's ability to direct their own play experiences, you can become better equipped to create environments and develop relationships that truly support all types of children's play. By following Pete's advice, you will be able to observe more carefully and knowledgeably before intervening, recognise and respond to children's play cues more sensitively and, ultimately, protect and preserve the play process more effectively.

As someone who has spent many years working with Early Years practitioners and educators around the world, I know how valuable this kind of practical theory can be. The Play Cycle gives you a language to describe what we observe in children's play, a framework to guide your practice and a way of assessing the effectiveness of your play environments for the children. Pete's book makes this powerful framework accessible to all, helping everyone enhance the quality of play experiences we offer to children, whatever type of setting you work in.

Whether you're studying for a qualification, developing your practice, or leading an Early Years setting, this book will expand your understanding of play and strengthen your ability to support it effectively. It's an essential resource for anyone committed to providing high-quality play experiences for children.

**Kathy Brodie**
Founder and host of Early Years TV

# ACKNOWLEDGMENTS

I want to acknowledge the following people who have helped shape this book: firstly, Dr Shelly Newstead, or Shelly who is my colleague, co-writer, co-researcher, and all-round good egg. I wish to thank Shelly for their contribution to the foreword.

Secondly, I want to thank Kathy Brodie for their contribution to the foreword and for being supportive of the Play Cycle through their Early Years TV. Kathy has helped promote the Play Cycle within the early years sector and has invited me on their Early Years TV on three occasions.

Thirdly, I want to thank Sarah Timmins who kindly and thoroughly read through each chapter and provided invaluable comments, edits, and amendments. The time they gave up reading through the draft book was very much appreciated.

Lastly, I want to thank Dawn Bunn, Rachel Dunne, Nikolai Koplewsky, Emma Sinclair, Rebekah Jackson Reece, and Tanya Petherrick for reading through Chapter 6 from respective Welsh, Republic of Ireland, Northern Ireland, Scottish, and English perspectives to help ensure regional accuracy. Again, the time given up was very much appreciated.

# GLOSSARY

| | |
|---|---|
| A | Adult |
| AIS | Adult Intervention Style |
| ADHD | Attention Deficit Hyperactivity Disorder |
| ASC | After School Club |
| AP | Adventure Playground |
| BA | Bachelor of Arts |
| CI | Care Inspectorate (Scotland) |
| CIW | Care Inspectorate Wales (Wales) |
| CAVS | Carmarthenshire Association of Voluntary Services |
| CGCHE | Cheltenham and Gloucestershire College for Higher Education |
| C&G | City & Guilds |
| CACHE | Council for Awards in Care, Health and Education |
| CCEA | Council for the Curriculum, Examinations and Assessment |
| CDT | Cognitive Development Theory |
| CoP | Community of Practice |
| CPD | Continuing Professional Development |
| DfE | Department for Education (UK Government) |
| DfEE | Department for Education and Employment (UK Government) |
| DoH | Department of Health |
| DoHSS | Department of Health and Social Services (Northern Ireland) |
| DPA | Developmental Play Assessment |
| DPT | Directive Play Therapy |
| ECEC | Early Childhood Education Centres |
| EYFS | Early Years Foundation Stage (England) |
| EYFSF | Early Years Foundation Stage Framework (England) |
| EST | Ecological Systems Theory |
| FCA | Fields of Constrained Action |
| FFA | Fields of Free Action |
| FPA | Fields of Promoted Action |
| FS | Forest Schools |
| GoI | Government of Ireland (RoI) |

| | |
|---|---|
| GOSH | Great Ormand Street Hospital |
| HSE | Health and Safety Executive |
| HSCT | Health and Social Care Trusts (Northern Ireland) |
| HNC | Higher National Certificate |
| HPS | Holiday Playschemes |
| IPA | International Play Association |
| ISB | Irish Statute Book (Republic of Ireland) |
| K | Knowledge (Skills, and Understanding) |
| LO | Learning Outcomes |
| LLP | Loose Parts Play |
| MPP | Mobile Play Provision |
| NCO | National Children's Office |
| NCCA | National Council for Curriculum and Assessment |
| NCFE | National Council for Further Education |
| NMS | National Minimum Standards |
| NDPP | Non-Directive Play Practice |
| NDPT | Non-Directive Play Therapy |
| NI | Northern Ireland |
| N-H | Non-Human |
| NOS | National Occupational Standards |
| N-TC | Non-Target Child |
| NPFA | National Playing Fields association (now Fields in Trust) |
| OFMDFM | Office for First Minister and Deputy First Minister (NI) |
| OMC | Office for Minister for Children (RoI) |
| OOSC | Out-of-School Club |
| P | Performance Criteria |
| P3 | Playwork Principles in Practice |
| PBL | Play-based Learning |
| PCOM | Play Cycle Observation Method |
| PT | Play Therapy |
| PPSG | Playwork Principles Scrutiny Group |
| PSA | Play Sufficiency Assessment |
| PGCE | Postgraduate Certificate in Education |
| PACT | Prison Advice Care Trust |
| PMLD | Profound and Multiple Learning Disabilities |
| RCIC | Reading Children's Information Centre |
| RAA | Resources, Application, and Analysis |
| R-BA | Risk-Benefit Analysis |
| RoI | Republic of Ireland |
| SCQF | Scottish Credit and Qualifications Framework |
| SG | Scottish Government |
| SQA | Scottish Qualifications Authority |
| SSSC | Scottish Social Services Council |
| SVQ | Scottish Vocational Qualifications |

| | |
|---|---|
| SSC | Sector Skills Council |
| SSO | Standard Setting Organisations |
| SCW | Social Care Wales |
| TC | Target Child |
| UK | United Kingdom |
| UN | United Nations |
| UNCRC | United Nations Convention on the Rights of the Child |
| UNICEF | United Nations International Children's Emergency Fund |
| UWCN | University of Wales College Newport |
| WAG | Welsh Assembly Government (now Welsh Government) |
| WG | Welsh Government |
| WJEC | Welsh Joint Education Committee |
| WAC | Wraparound Care |
| ZPD | Zone of Proximal Development |

# Introduction

## The Play Cycle: how it all began

## Introduction

The Play Cycle began as a conference paper at the International Play Association Conference (IPA) in Colorado, USA, and was delivered by the late Gordon Sturrock and the late Professor Perry Else in 1998 (Sturrock & Else, 1998). The conference paper titled 'The Playground as Therapeutic Space: Playwork as Healing' more commonly referred to as the 'Colorado Paper' introduced a new theory of play – The Play Cycle. Now, 27 years later, the Play Cycle is the central topic of this book. This Introductory chapter begins with a personal reflection on how the Play Cycle has shaped my professional and academic career. This chapter then considers how the Play Cycle focuses on the process of play and the different types of play environments where play happens, and where the Play Cycle can be applied. The chapter concludes with the structure of the book.

## A personal reflection on the Play Cycle

This very brief resume outlines how my 'life' in play and playwork, from an accidental beginning in 1996 to the current day, has been accompanied by the Play Cycle. I fell into the world of play and playwork in June 1996 when I was asked to help out at an After-School Club (ASC) in Oxford, shortly after completing my Postgraduate Certificate in Education (PGCE) in secondary school science. A year later I was running the ASC and soon after was employed by the Reading Children's Information Centre (RCIC) to run an Out-of-School Club (OOSC) project in Wokingham funded by the then United Kingdom (UK) Government's Department for Education and Employment (DfEE). It was when running this latter project that I first came across the Play Cycle although I did not start to become fully involved with using it in my practice until I became the Play Development Officer for Cheltenham Borough Council in 2000. Here I delivered 'Take 10 for Play' (Stobart, 1998) for the organisation Playwork Partnerships based within the Cheltenham and Gloucestershire College of Higher Education (CGCHE) (now the University of Gloucestershire) which included the Play Cycle in the course material.

In 2002, I moved to Wales, and in took up the position of lecturer on the Playwork Pathway for the BA Community Studies course at the University College of Wales Newport (UCWN), now the University of South Wales. The Play Cycle formed the basis of the play element for the programme and I taught on the course until 2006 when I went on to work for Pembrokeshire County Council as their Project Officer responsible for developing play within the local authority and delivering training to the childcare sector. The main training I delivered was on the Play Cycle including continuing professional development workshops which introduced the Play Cycle to childcare workers and childminders. I remained in this post until 2008 when I left to take up the post as the Play Development Manager for the BIG Lottery-funded project to develop play across Pembrokeshire and Carmarthenshire with the Carmarthenshire Association of Voluntary Services (CAVS). I was in this post for six months before leaving to undertake my PhD researching children's perception of choice in their play.

In 2012, whilst writing up my PhD, I returned to work for CAVS as their Project Officer to run the BIG Lottery Play Project in Pembrokeshire which involved the recruiting and training of a playwork team to facilitate play in children's local parks and open spaces. The training, as before, included the Play Cycle, with the focus on play sessions being child-led (King & Sills-Jones, 2018). The ethos of this project, as with other outdoor play projects, is summed up by this comment from one playworker on how the Play Cycle has changed their practice:

> Setting up a range of resources, equipment and activities for an open play session on a neighbourhood park, to allow freely chosen, child led play.
>
> Playworker

In 2013, I left the project to take up my current role at Swansea University lecturing on the MA Developmental and Therapeutic Play course. I have researched the Play Cycle with my colleague Dr Shelly Newstead (King & Newstead, 2019; 2020) and co-authored a book with the late Gordon Sturrock (King & Sturrock, 2019). I have also developed an observational tool to record the Play Cycle, the Play Cycle Observational Method (PCOM) (King, 2020b). More recently, I have added to the theory of the Play Cycle (King, 2023; 2024). In addition to using the Play Cycle in my professional practice, I have delivered it in workshops, induction sessions, conferences, lectures, and continuing professional development. The Play Cycle over the last 30 years forms the basis of this book

## Defining play

> Play is behavior which itself satisfies a motive. It is performed for its own sake, rather than as a means to reaching some "goal" in the ordinary sense of the word. In other words, the behaviour itself is the goal.
>
> (Slotkin, 1950, p. 271)

This definition of play, which is not the only definition to be found in the literature, was found in a book published in 1950 on 'Social Anthropology' (Slotkin, 1950).

> **Reflective Question:**
>
> What are your thoughts on this definition of play?
>
> How does it stand the 'test of time'

Defining play has been, and continues to be, a highly debatable and conflicting argument. From the 19th-century classical theorists (Groos, 1901; Hall, 1905) through the 20th-century developmental psychologists (Piaget, 1952; Vygotsky, 1978) to the current perspectives (Garvey, 1990), play has been defined within educational, therapeutic, and recreational play practice (Howard & McInnes, 2013). Play has been defined within types, categories, and criteria (Howard, 2002) reflecting the seven types of rhetoric (the speech or writing intended to be effective and influence people) put forward by Sutton-Smith (1997). However play is defined, Hughes (2002) considered it to be 'the behavioural and psychic equivalent of oxygen' (p. xxiii).

Play defined as categories or types considers how the nature of play changes over time. An example of this is Piaget's (1952) three types of play: pretend; symbolic, and games with rules that are aligned to their Cognitive Development Theory (CDT) (Barrouillet, 2015). Vygotsky (1978) recognised the importance of play in cognitive development concerning the Zone of Proximal Development (ZPD) where children are scaffolded (Wood et al., 1976) from their actual level to their potential level by more able peers. The more able peers could be either adults or peers. When considering social play, Parten (1932) proposed six social categories within social play: unoccupied, onlooker, solitary, parallel, associative, and co-operative. Sandseter (2009a) proposed six types of risky play: great heights; high speed; dangerous tools; dangerous elements; rough and tumble, and disappearing or getting lost. Defining play as a category or type is based on an outcome on what is observed, however, it is often difficult to reduce any observed play to one category or type. Hughes's (2001) 'Taxonomy of Play Types' puts forward 16 different types of play but to narrow this down to a single type of play is difficult. For example, when a child, or group of children play football, a number of types of play are apparent, with no single type dominant; physical play (the children are moving vigorously), object play (the football), and games with rules (football has clear rules, for example, the off-side rule).

Play defined by criteria consists of principles or standards by which something may be judged or decided as reflected in Slotkin's (1950) statement 'society categories play on the basis of its mores. Play which is right is recreation; play which is wrong is vice' (p. 282). Rubin et al. (1983) put forward a definition of play based on five criteria: intrinsic motivation, free choice, pleasurable, non-literal, and active engagement. Garvey (1977) proposed a definition of play with four criteria: enjoyable, no extrinsic goals, spontaneous, and active engagement. Krasnor and Pepler (1980) provide another criteria of play, that of flexibility, positive affect, nonliterality, means/ends, and intrinsic motivation. Do all the criteria have to be present for something to be considered as play? Smith and Voldstedt's (1985) study of the Krasnor and Pepler (1980) criteria found reasonable agreement from 70 observers, there was better agreement for flexibility, positive affect, and nonliterally compared to means/end and intrinsic motivation. Smith and Vollstedt (1985) suggest that means/end and intrinsic motivation are less likely to be observed.

Whether using a category, type or criteria approach, defining play will often depend on the context in which it is being used, implemented, or facilitated and the most used definition that reflects theory (Garvey, 1977), policy (Welsh Government (WG), 2002; Scottish Government (SG), 2013) and practice (Playwork Principles Scrutiny Group (PPSG), 2005). The most commonly used definition of play is 'Play is freely chosen, intrinsically motivated for no external goal' (National Playing Fields Association (NPFA) et al., 2000), which does not deviate much from the definition at the start of this chapter. However, it has been argued that play is not always freely chosen (King & Howard, 2014) or intrinsically motivated for no external goal (Brown, 2008).

Whilst there is never going to be a universal definition or agreement of play, Neumann (1971) offered a 'hypothetical definition of play' that consists of three elements of criteria, process, and objectives:

- The **criteria** of play are intrinsic motivation, internal reality, and internal locus of control of the activity
- Play is a **process** that has modes and operations.
- Play is directed towards **objectives**: objects, subjects, functions and location.

This 'hypothetical definition of play' is a good starting point when considering child-led play and the Play Cycle. The criteria focus on children's internal world, and their choice to initiate or end play. The process reflects the Play Cycle as this focuses on the process of play. Objectives relate to the external world, the loose parts in the play environment. The focus on the 'process' enables the Play Cycle to be used within a recreational (playwork or childcare) setting, in a therapeutic context, and within early years education.

## The process of play

The theory and application of the Play Cycle focuses on the process of play (King & Newstead, 2020, 2021c, 2022a; King & Sturrock, 2019; Sturrock & Else, 1998) rather than an outcome. The process of play in the Play Cycle consists of six elements: pre-cue; play cue; play return; play frame; flow; and annihilation – an established Play Cycle may last from a second to hours. The importance of focusing on the process of play is that Play Cycles can be observed and recorded wherever play is taking place and who is involved in the Play Cycle. Irrespective of different perceptions of play, for example between adults and children (McInnes et al., 2011; 2013) and between typical and atypically developing children (Eisele & Howard, 2012), Play Cycles can be reliably observed and recorded (King et al., 2021). The Play Cycle can support professional play practice in any context and can be also used to support play where it may be focused on outcomes.

## The different types of play environments

The Play Cycle and the Play Cycle Observation Method outlined within this book can be used and applied to any context where children play. This can range from home to school, from the street to the ASC. Many ASCs and Holiday Playschemes (HPS) use school premises outside of the school curricula (King, 2020; 2021b) and this can include Wraparound Care (WAC) (Holloway & Pimlott-Wilson, 2017) all under the broad term as Out-of-School Clubs (OOSC). The following list is not definitive, but shows the diversity of potential play spaces where children and young people play:

- Adventure Playgrounds (AP)
- After-School Club (ASC)

- Holiday Playscheme (HPS)
- Mobile Play Projects in parks and open spaces (MPP)
- Nurseries
- Day Care
- Wraparound Care WAC
- Pre-School and Playgroups
- Schools (both primary and secondary)
- Forest School
- Childminders
- Hospitals
- Prisons
- Others that have not been listed

How children play within and between these different types of context and provision have one thing in common; the process of play. Differences include whether the provision is open access or closed access. Open access play is evidenced in adventure playgrounds (King, 2021a) and mobile play projects in children's local parks and open spaces (King & Sills-Jones, 2015) and is defined as when, 'Children are not restricted in their movements, other than where related to safety matters and are not prevented from coming and going as and they wish' (Welsh Government, 2014, p. 38). The alternative to open access is closed access, for example, WAC, ASC, and HPS (King, 2022a) where children have to remain within the setting for the designated period they have been booked in for. When attending an ASC, children either make their way to the club or are collected from their class by one of the ASC staff. For the holiday playschemes, children arrive and are collected by a parent or carer.

Play is also used within the primary education curricula (McInnes, 2021) and this can include play-based learning (Pyle & Danniels, 2017). Play is also used within Forest Schools (FS) (Maynard, 2007) where outdoor play is promoted along with risky play (Garden & Downes, 2023). Outdoor play within primary schools occurs during break times and recess although the amount of time spent playing outside in primary school has declined (Baines & Blatchford, 2019).

Play is also used in therapeutic contexts for example in hospitals and prisons. For children who experience both short-term and long-term stays in hospitals, play is often used as a distraction in pre-operational procedures (Haiat et al., 2003; Koukourikos et al., 2015), recovery (Çelebi et al, 2015) and providing an outlet for fear and anxiety (Jun-Tai, 2008; Salmi & Hanson, 2021). The child could be playing in a specialist playroom, or the play could be confined to their bed. The play will often involve the hospital play specialist (Webster, 2000) whose play practice can support how children 'normally' play at home or play that is planned to reduce the fear and anxiety of potential medical procedures (Perasso et al., 2021). Many hospitals have play specialists working within the children's wards, for example, Great Ormand Street Hospital (GOSH) in London and Morriston Hospital in Swansea.

Another therapeutic context for play is the visits made by children to parents (usually the father) in prisons (Quaintrell, 2021). Setting up opportunities for play between children and parents provides a more relaxed environment that enhances the quality of visiting time (Woodall & Kinsella, 2017). An example of this is the national charity Prison Advice and Care Trust (PACT) working with families across England and Wales.

## The structure of the book

The book is divided into distinct chapters which cover a specific topic related to the Play Cycle. Each chapter includes 'reflective questions' that enable the reader to consider the Play Cycle and topic discussed with their knowledge and understanding in conjunction with their practice and/or study. Each chapter also includes short vignettes from playworkers, childcare workers, and early years workers. These vignettes originated from four sources. The first source was an online survey undertaken by King and Newstead (2020) on playworkers' understanding of the Play Cycle. Within this study, participants were asked how they have used the Play Cycle in practice. The second vignette source was another online survey by King and Newstead (2022b), this time exploring childcare workers' understanding of the Play Cycle. As with the first online study, childcare workers were asked how they have used the Play Cycle in practice. The third source was the International Playwork Census undertaken by King and Newstead (2022b) where participants provided examples of using the Play Cycle in their practice. The fourth source were from students from Swansea University reflecting on using the Play Cycle on their placements. Vignettes from these three studies and the student placements are used throughout the book.

Chapter 1 provides an update and overview of the Play Cycle. This includes the revised definitions of the six elements of the Play Cycle: pre-cue, play cue, play return, play frame, flow, and annihilation (King & Newstead; King & Sturrock, 2019) and the development of the theory (King, 2022; 2023). The chapter concludes with the PCOM (King, 2021) that can be used to record the process of play and is explained in more detail in Chapter 5.

Chapter 2 considers the play environment and how children interact with both the indoor and outdoor spaces. This interaction includes the theories of affordances (Gibson, 1986) and loose parts (Nicholson, 1971) and how they are important to enable all types of play to take place (Whitebread et al., 2012).

Chapter 3 begins with an overview of the United Nations Convention of the Child (UNCRC) (United Nations International Children's Emergency Fund (UNICEF), 2019) with a specific focus on Article 31, the right to play. The chapter then considers child-led play and how it differs from child-initiated, child-centered, and child-directed play. Child-led play is discussed in relation to non-directive play (Axline, 1947) and the importance of risk (Dodd & Lester, 2021).

Chapter 5 covers the intervention styles that enable adults to support the process of play. The different intervention styles described are play maintenance, simple involvement, medial intervention, and complex intervention (Sturrock & Else, 1998; Sturrock et al., 2004). How the intervention styles are positioned concerning the Play Cycle is explained. The chapter considers how the Play Cycle and the four intervention styles could be used within play-based learning (Bergen, 1988; Pyle & Danniels, 2017; Weisberg et al., 2013). Chapter 5 concludes with how the Play Cycle, and the PCOM can be used by practitioners within reflective practice.

Chapter 6 provides an update on the Play Cycle Observation Method (King, 2021; King & Sturrock, 2019) using the RAA approach of Resources, Application, and Analysis. How to use the PCOM is explained in detail; the resources can be found in the appendices.

The book concludes with an overview of topics discussed in the previous chapters. The conclusion chapter considers the potential challenges of using the Play Cycle regarding policy and legislation, vocational qualifications, professional practice, and individual perceptions of play. The book concludes with the 'Colorado Paper' (Sturrock & Else, 1998), which was where the Play Cycle was first imagined and describes how any adult involved in children's play can used the Play Cycle to support the process of play.

## Conclusion

This book aims to inform the practitioner, the student, and the student-practitioner to support their professional practice and learning in supporting and reflecting on children's play. Throughout each chapter, there are reflective questions to consider and vignettes from playworkers, childcare workers, and early years workers on how the Play Cycle has been used in professional practice. I hope you enjoy reading the book and find it useful in your studies, your practice, or hopefully in both contexts.

# 1 The Play Cycle revised and updated

## Introduction

This chapter provides an overview of the background to the Play Cycle, the six elements that make it up, and how adults can support Play Cycles. Since its introduction in 1998, the Play Cycle has been further researched (King & Newstead, 2020; 2021; 2022) and the theory developed (King, 2022b; 2023), enabling a deeper understanding, and more effective recording, of how children play. Developing an understanding of the Play Cycle will support students in achieving the relevant standards for the playwork, childcare, or early years qualifications being studied and will support playworkers and early years care and education workers in their practice. For more detailed information on the research undertaken and theory written about the Play Cycle since 1998, refer to the references at the end of the chapter.

## Where it all began

In 1998, at the International Play Association (IPA) Conference in Colorado, USA, Gordon Sturrock and Perry Else delivered a presentation titled 'The playground as therapeutic space: playwork as healing', which became known more affectionately as 'The Colorado Paper' (Sturrock & Else, 1998). 'The Colorado Paper' (Sturrock & Else, 1998) was summed up by King and Sturrock (2019):

> The 'Colorado Paper' is a very deep and complex paper, one of those cases where you can read and re-read it and something new will always appear. The paper proposes at the onset the "natural space for play (both physical and psychic) is steadily being eroded, where the playful habit – or more widely what we describe as the ludic ecology – is being curtailed or contaminated, we see increasing signs of breakdown and dis-ease" (p. 74). The 'Colorado Paper' considers play practice from a more "interpretive and analytical perspective …. termed psycholudics, the study of the mind or psyche at play" (p. 76), where the playworker "develops insights and interpretative responses" (p. 77) to the content and meaning of children's play. Sturrock and Else (1998) put forward that playworkers, as with therapists and analysts, are in a position to understand the content and meaning of children's play from a therapeutic perspective. This therapeutic perspective is considered with reference to the work of the Czech psychiatrist Stanislav Grof, who was one of the founders of transpersonal psychology; the paediatrician and psychoanalyst

Donald W. Winnicott who, introduced the concept of the transitional object; Ken Wilber, a philosopher and writer on transpersonal psychology; and the Swiss psychiatrist and psychoanalyst Carl Gustav Jung.

(p. 14)

Within this conference presentation, Sturrock and Else (1988) outlined the process of play called 'The Play Cycle' and how adults can support it (see King & Sturrock, 2019 for a more detailed background of the Play Cycle). Since the introduction of 'The Colorado Paper' in 1998, the Play Cycle has underpinned professional playwork practice within the 'Playwork Principles' (Playwork Principle Scrutiny Group (PPSG), 2005) and the National Occupational Standards (NOS) for playwork. The Play Cycle has undergone a revision (King & Newstead, 2019), and the theoretical grounding has been expanded (King, 2022b; 2023).

## Revising and updating the Play Cycle

In 2018, when the Play Cycle was 20 years old, King and Newstead undertook two studies to explore the understanding of the Play Cycle as described in 'The Colorado Paper': one study was with playworkers (2020) and one with childcare workers (2022). The six elements of the original Play Cycle detailed in the 'Colorado Paper' were the meta-lude, play cue, play return, play frame, loop and flow, and annihilation; these were included as individual questions in both the surveys and participants were asked to write down their understanding of each element (King & Newstead, 2019, 2022). It was clear from both studies that the meta-lude was not understood, and whilst flow appeared clear, the aspect of loop was not. The analysis from both studies resulted in a revision of the six elements of the Play Cycle and provided a clear definition for each (King & Newstead, 2020; King & Sturrock, 2019). The six elements of the Play Cycle are now the pre-cue (replaced the meta-lude), play cue, play return, play frame, flow (replaced loop and flow), and annihilation. The definition of each element, with specific examples, are shown below:

### *Pre-cue*

A conscious or unconscious thought or idea within the child's inner world which may result in the issue of a play cue. For example, a child has an urge to play with a ball and tennis racket.

### *Play cue*

A verbal or non-verbal action from a person or object in the child's 'outer world' responding to the play cue. The child may ask another child to play with the tennis ball and racket with them (sends out a play cue).

### *Play return*

A verbal or non-verbal action from a person or object in the child's 'outer world' responding to the play cue. The other child agrees to play (the play return), and they get another racket and start hitting the ball to each other (this forms the Play Cycle).

## Play frame

The visible (physical) or imagined (non-physical) boundary that keeps the Play Cycle intact for the play to continue. The two children are hitting the ball to each other on a grass rectangle piece of turf. This rectangle area acts as the play frame.

## Flow

Where play cues and play returns are continually being processed between the child's 'inner and outer world' resulting in the child appearing 'lost' in their play. As the two children continue to hit the ball to each other, they forget about time and where they are, they are 'lost' in their play, or in flow within the established Play Cycle. Play cues and play returns may continue to happen in flow, for example, one child may say 'close your eyes' and then hit the ball to the other child.

## Annihilation

The play has finished where an element of the Play Cycle, or the play frame, has no interest to the child. Eventually, the Play Cycle comes to an end; it may be that one of the children gets bored and puts their racket down and walks off. The Play Cycle has finished or annihilated.

The purpose of revising the six elements of the Play Cycle each with a clear definition was to enable consistency of interpretation and subsequent use in professional practice (King & Newstead, 2020), not just within playwork but any professional practice that uses the Play Cycle, for example, childcare and early years education (King & Newstead, 2022).

# Developing the theory behind the Play Cycle

The Play Cycle was initially developed by Sturrock and Else (1998) and included concepts from other disciplines which include transpersonal psychology, and psychoanalysis (King & Sturrock, 2019). The six elements of the Play Cycle can be linked to other concepts and theories: for example, the play cue can be traced back to Bateson's (1955) study of primates in the 1950s, the play frame relates to Goffman's (1974) concept of 'Frame Analysis' and flow is a psychological concept developed by Csikszentmihalyi (1975). While the Play Cycle describes the process of play, the theory has been further developed concerning the two unobservable elements of the Play Cycle, the pre-cue and flow. The pre-cue, or idea to play, has been linked to the concept of the 'Functional Cycle' (von Uexküll, 1982; 2010) and the concept of 'affordances' (Gibson, 1986) and Nicholson's (1971) theory of 'loose parts'. The concept of Flow (Csikszentmihalyi, 1975) has been developed concerning the 'potential space' or 'third area' (Winnicott, 1972) and links in with the four hierarchal levels of Adult Intervention Styles (AIS) to support the Play Cycle.

The pre-cue is the thought or idea to play which is internal to the child and contained within their inner world. The pre-cue cannot be observed. The pre-cue, however, can be stimulated through the child's senses by the objects and people in their outer world. The objects can be both natural and those made by humans. The stimulation of external objects has been explained as the 'external perceptual cue' based on von Uexküll's concept of the

Functional Cycle (King, 2022b). The external objects in the surrounding environments, in particular those the child or children can manipulate are described as 'loose parts' (Nicholson, 1971). More 'loose parts' available to the child results in more potential external perceptual cues to stimulate the pre-cue (the idea to play). How the child perceives the external perceptual cue and how they want to manipulate the objects in their play relates to the concept of affordances (Gibson, 1985).

When a Play Cycle forms, play cues continued to be issued, which may or may not get a play return, to keep the Play Cycle going. This can be termed as an 'established Play Cycle' (King, 2023). As the established Play Cycle continues with play cues and returns, children become 'lost' in their play and they forget all notion of time and space. This is what Czikesnehhaiyi (1975) referred to as flow. Flow is not observable, it is something we experience, but other children and adults *can* play a part in the flow of established Play Cycles (King, 2023). Whilst the pre-cue and flow cannot be observed, these two elements of the Play Cycle have been developed from the theory originally put forward by Sturrock and Else (1998).

## The adult role in the Play Cycle

The adult role in the Play Cycle is to support the process of play (King & Strurrock, 2019; King & Newstead, 2021a; 2021b; Sturrock & Else, 1998) and not to take over and control it for adult agendas, or what Sturrock and Else (1998) termed 'adulteration'. Adulteration is where the Play Cycle is used for an adult-focused objective, rather than children directing the purpose of their play themselves.

The adult can support the process of play in one of four ways termed AIS: play maintenance, simple involvement, medial intervention, and complex intervention (Sturrock & Else, 1998; Sturrock et al., 2004):

- **Play Maintenance** - The play is self-contained - no intervention is necessary; the worker observes the activity.
- **Simple Involvement** - The adult acts as a resource for the play - this may be subtle, as in making a tool available for use, or more overt, responding to a request from children.
- **Medial Intervention** - At the request of the child, the adult becomes involved in the play - such as by offering alternatives from which the child chooses, or by initiating a game then withdrawing.
- **Complex Intervention** - There is a direct and extended overlap between playing children and the adult - the adult may need to take on a role in the play, or act as a partner to the playing child.

For the adult practitioner, it is possible to be in more than one of these AIS levels of hierarchy at the same time. The practitioner is often observing other children's Play Cycles whilst being an active participant in one. Whether in play maintenance, simple involvement, medial intervention, or complex intervention, the adult aims to keep the Play Cycles intact within the play frame where they have a containment role (Sturrock & Else, 1998). The adult role in the Play Cycle is covered in more detail in Chapter 4.

## 12  The Play Cycle in practice

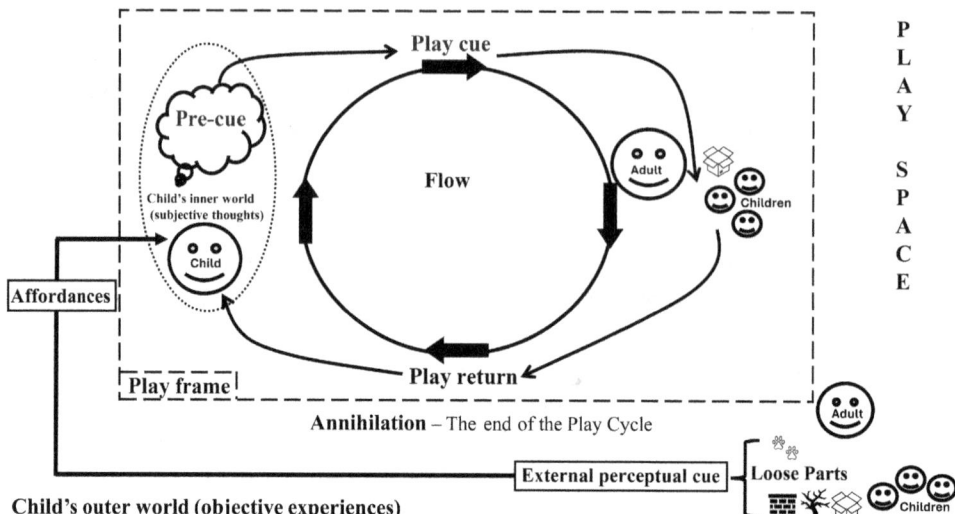

Figure 1.1  An updated version of the Play Cycle

## A summary of the Play Cycle

Figure 1.1 is an updated version of the Play Cycle (pre-cue, play cue, play return, play frame, flow, and annihilation) where the pre-cue (child's inner world) can be stimulated by an object in the outside world as an external perceptual cue. The key aspects are:

- The external perceptual cue can stimulate the idea to play (pre-cue) which can be from a person or an object in the child's external world.
- The pre-cue is internal to the child and cannot be observed.
- The play cue is issued to the child's external world.
- The play return can be from another person or an object.
- The state of flow cannot be observed, however, play cues and returns continue within an established Play Cycle that contributes to flow.
- The adult has a containing role in keeping the play frame intact.

> **Reflective Question:**
>
> Reflect on your professional practice with examples where you have been involved in the Play Cycle. Were you supporting the process of play, or were you taking charge (adulteration)?

## Examples of the Play Cycle being used in practice

King & Newstead (2019; 2020) asked playworkers and childcare workers about their understanding of the Play Cycle. Below are comments provided on how playworkers, childcare workers, and early years workers have used the Play Cycle in practice:

> The Play cycle has enabled us to intervene with children on a more subtle level. Especially those children whose play cues tended to be on the more "aggressive" side, to help them develop a clearer frame for their play, which they were happy with. This encouraged their play cues to be less aggressive and initiated a play return.
>
> Playworker
>
> Makes me more aware of stepping back and observing play. Makes me not worry that I should appear to be having some sort of interaction with the children all the time, but to let them play freely without imposing my ideas on them, either intentionally or unintentionally.
>
> Childcare Worker
>
> Working in Early Years gives me the opportunity to observe play in the best resourced area of the school.
>
> Early Years Workers
>
> We use an awareness of the Play Cycle, and the related theories of adult interventions, to run our sessions. It affects how we observe the children, how we resource our sessions, how we communicate with children, and how we behave ourselves. Awareness of the Play Cycle helps play space design, through observing Play Cycles and where they happen.
>
> Forest School (FS) Worker.

Since the Play Cycle was first introduced in 1998 by Gordon Sturrock and Perry Else at the IPA in Colorado, USA, it has become ingrained within professional practice, training, and education within playwork (King & Newstead, 2021b; 2024). It has also been recognised in childcare and early years practice. The definitions of the six elements of the Play Cycle (pre-cue, play cue, play return, play frame, flow, and annihilation) have been revised and updated based on current practitioners' understanding of the Play Cycle. In addition, the theory of the Play Cycle has been updated to include the theory of loose parts (Nicholson, 1971), affordances (Gibson, 1986), the Functional Cycle (Uexküll, 1982; 2010), and Flow (Csikszentmihalyi, 1975).

## Observing and recording the Play Cycle

This chapter has provided an up-to-date account of the theory of the Play Cycle. The Play Cycle has also been developed to be used as an observational tool that records elements of the process of play (King, 2020b). This is known as the Play Cycle Observation Method (PCOM) and this is explained in detail in Chapter 5. The PCOM, in addition to being used as an observational tool, can also be used as part of professional reflective practice that can support practitioners undertaking professional qualifications linked to the NOS within playwork, childcare, and early years.

When relating the Play Cycle to the NOS (or equivalent) of vocational courses, the following factors need to be considered: Play Environment, Resources and Activities, Child-Centred, AIS, and Theory:

- How is the play space set up for Play Cycles to take place?
- What resources and activities are available to enable different types of play?

- How is child-initiated/child-led/child-centred/child-directed play being facilitated?
- What AIS is being used to support Play Cycles?
- How can the theory of the Play Cycle support other theories?
- How can the Play Cycle be used to undertake observations of play?
- How can the Play Cycle be used within reflective practice?

These questions will be answered in the following chapters on the play environment, child-led play, the adult role in supporting the process of play, and the policy and practice.

## Conclusion

This chapter provides an up-to-date account of the Play Cycle theory and the re-defined six elements that make it up: pre-cue, play cue, play return, play frame, flow, and annihilation. How adults can support the Play Cycle is described within the four hierarchal levels of intervention: play maintenance, simple involvement, medial intervention, and complex intervention.

The Play Cycle can support practitioners, students, or those who are both students and practitioners undertaking vocational-related qualifications. The Play Cycle can be applied to key NOS areas of the play environment, child-centred, AIS, theory, and reflective practice. These key areas are found within vocational courses in playwork, childcare, and early years, and are covered in the following chapters.

---

**Further Reading**

For more detailed information on the research undertaken and the developing theory of the Play Cycle, the following reading is suggested:

- King, P., & Newstead, S. (2020). Re-defining the Play Cycle: An Empirical Study of Playworkers' Understanding of Playwork Theory. Journal of Early Childhood Research, 18(1), 99-111.
- King, P. (2022). A Theoretical Expansion off the Play Cycle: Jakob von Uexküll's Functional Cycle and the Perceptual Cue. American Journal of Play, 14(1), 173-187.
- King, P. (2023). Flow and the Play Cycle: A Theoretical Consideration of the Importance of Flow in Established Play Cycles. American Journal of Play, 15(2), 197-195.

---

**Video Resources**

The Play Cycle is explained concisely in the following videos:

- https://youtu.be/2Qfqjy4IHr0?si=tmSPFbXDfl9RcaQM.
- https://youtu.be/u2tdfRzfKjM?si=7c3ubi69oBKyfsyM. (with subtitles)

# 2 The Play Cycle and the play environment

## Introduction

The play environment needs to appeal to children to play as set out by the seven play objectives within 'Best Play' (National Playing Fields Association (NPFA) et al., 2000). This chapter continues to explore the interaction of the child with the environment and considers von Uexküll's (1982; 2010) Functional Cycle, Gibson's (1986) concept of affordances, and Kyttä's (2004) Fields of Free Action (FFA). The objects within the play environments are discussed regarding to Nicholson's (1971) theory of 'Loose Parts' and the chapter concludes with a consideration of the different types of play children can engage in within the play environment. These are all discussed and linked to the Play Cycle.

## The play environment or the 'Ludic ecology'

The play environment, or play space is a 'transferable and loose notion that can be applied to any environment in which a child chooses to play' (Woolley & Lowe, 2013, p. 54). The play environment will most often consists of:

- An area to play that may be as small as a designated area on a housing estate (and these can be small) or a room within a primary school.
- An area to play that may be as large as a field where you can just about see the 'other side', a dedicated area to play such as an Adventure Playground (AP), or a room in a school, for example, an After School Club (ASC).
- The fixed objects that cannot be moved, for example, a metal climbing frame or a tree.
- Objects that are flexible enough to destroy or create, for example, a cardboard box or a branch.
- Other people, children, young people and adults.
- Other species, for example, worms or larger animals such as dogs.

Sturrock and Else (1998) referred to the interaction of the child's inner world or 'internalised play space' (p. 83) with the external world as the 'ludic ecology' (p. 83). The ludic ecology, they assert is a fluid projection of ideas that constantly changes as the child's play adapts to the environment. The ludic ecology, as with basic ecological principles, refers to the study of 'organisms or groups of organisms to their environment' (Odum, 1971, p. 3). In this respect, the groups of organisms are children, and the environment is the play environment.

Vickerius and Sandberg (2004) consider two aspects of the play environment. The first is the physical environment (the surroundings) and the second is the social environment (an individual child, other children, and adults). The combination of the physical, social, and emotional environment can be inferred from Russell's (2012) conceived, perceived, and lived space based on Lefebvre's (1991) spatial triad. Russell (2012) explains the conceived space as the mental space of adults (cartographers, planners, and architects). The perceived space is the everyday routine of life as experienced through the senses, and the lived space is the moment of escape, the space to play. As Russell (2012) stated:

> Regarding rules and relationships is to do with how issues of power and resistance play out in Lefebvre's lived space. Rules are devised in conceived space, implemented or not through spatial practice, and resisted in lived space.
>
> (Russell, 2012, p. 60)

Children's Play Cycles will contain the conceived, perceived, and lived space within the ecological perspective of the play environment. The interaction of the child and the environment links to the Play Cycle when considering the concept of the Functional Cycle (von Uexküll, 1982, p. 2010).

> **Reflective Question**
>
> How would you describe the 'ecology' of the play space you currently work in?

## The Play Cycle and the Functional Cycle

von Uexküll's (1982, p. 2010) Functional Cycle is based on the interaction of animals and their surrounding environment. von Uexküll called this interaction an umwelt (von Uexküll 1982, p. 2010). The umwelt is an organism's subjective experience within the objective environment (Feiten, 2020). When children play, their exists a subjective inner world (which we can't see) and an objective outer world where they interact with the environment (which we can see). The umwelt can be viewed as the child's subjective play experience in the objective play space where the Play Cycle begins. It starts within the child's inner world as the pre-cue that issues a play cue to the outer world. If there is a play return in the outer world, this is returned to the child's inner world.

In von Uexküll's (1982, p. 2010) Functional Cycle, the objects in the environment provide perceptual cues that the environment offers to an organism. The external objects within the environment von Uexküll referred to as 'meaning carriers'. The external object is perceived by an organism, however the 'meaning' of the object will differ depending on what it offers. For example, a blade of grass in a field may offer a 'meaning' of resting for a grasshopper, but for a sheep, it could be a source of food. The meaning carrier, if picked up as a perceptual cue enters the organism's subject inner world as a 'meaning receiver' and may result in an effect provided, for example, the sheep starts to eat the grass. When considering children's play, the

*The Play Cycle and the play environment* 17

'meaning receiver' will be perceived through the five senses (what Von Uexküll termed the perceptual organ) and this may stimulate the pre-cue (the idea to play) and issue a play cue. The play cue is what von Uexküll called the 'effector'. von Uexküll (1982) suggests that each object carries a meaning perceived by an animal but influenced by the environment and its contents.

Concerning the Play Cycle, the perceptual cue from the objective outer world will have different meanings on how and if children want to play. For example, a cardboard box (meaning carrier) is spotted by a child (a perceptual cue) which stimulates the pre-cue for an idea to play with it (meaning receiver). The child issues a play cue to get the box (effector) and sits in it. The child uses the box as a seat. For another child, they may see the box and instead of sitting in it, they may choose to jump on it to play. The same object (cardboard box) offers different meanings to the children for how they want to play. von Uexküll's Umwelt and meaning carrier have the same properties as the affordances developed by Gibson (1986).

> **Reflective Question**
>
> What perceptual cues can you list in your play environment that may stimulate an idea to play?

## The play environment and affordances

Affordances refer to the relationship between an organism and its environment and specifically what the environment can offer it (Gibson, 1986). Heft (2003) noted that as with the Functional Cycle (van Uexküll, 1982; 2010), what and how an organism perceives the environment will vary where:

> At a minimum, affordances are specified relative to an individual. More than that, however, affordance meaning is also typically established by a feature's relation to a broader environmental context. This claim is most easily supported with reference to cases where the same object can have different functional meanings in different environmental contexts.
>
> (Heft, 2003, p. 172)

This variation relates to the different types of affordances that exist. The different types of affordances are structural affordances (the objects in the environment that are not changeable); functional affordances (the activities and resources found in the environment); social affordances (termed the people within the environment); and emotional affordances (termed how people feel in the environment) (Costall, 1995; Heft, 2003; Hyvönen & Juujärvi, 2005; Isbister et al., 2018; King & Howard, 2014; Kyttä, 2002). The physical environment reflects the structural and functional affordances whilst the social environment encompasses social affordances. However, concerning emotional affordances, a third aspect could be added which is the emotional environment which can be considered as the subjective experience of the physical and social environment.

Kyttä's (2002; 2004) study on children's mobility and access to outdoor spaces considered the potential affordances from the environment that are perceived and used by children. The perceived affordances that are used by the child can shape the environment. The potential and used affordances have three types of Fields: Fields of Free Action (FFA), Fields of Promoted Action (FPA), and Fields of Constrained Action (FCA) (Kyttä, 2002).

The FFA is where the child or children have the most use of the potential affordances that is in their choice. The FPA and FCA are influenced by social and cultural norms which can promote, or limit the potential use of affordances. The promotion of affordances is termed the FPA and the restriction of affordances is termed the FCA. For example, social norms may encourage social play (FPA) but prevent play risky play (FCA). The FPA and the FCA will influence the FFA. The association of potential and used affordances has been classified by Kyttä (2002, 2004) into four main groups:

- Bullerby: A high level of used affordances where the FFA dominates, supported by FPA, and a low FCA. For example, an Adventure Playground.
- Glasshouse: A high level of used affordances where the FCA dominates over the FFA and FPA. For example, ASC or Holiday Playscheme (HPS).
- Wasteland: A low level of used affordances where the FFA dominates, supported by the FPA, and a low level of FCA. For example, a run-down park with limited, broken, or no resources.
- Cell: A low level of used affordances where the FCA dominates over the FFA and the FPA. For example, access to the street directly outside of the house that is full of parked cars.

The FFA, FPA, and FCA can be reflected in the Play Cycle. With the FFA, where the child or children have the most control over their play, the used affordances will offer more opportunities for different types of play to take place providing the play space is adequately resourced. Within the FPA, this can reflect the adult role in the Play Cycle and the four levels of intervention: play maintenance, simple involvement, medial intervention, and complex intervention. When considering the FCA, this can be linked to the aspect of adulteration (for levels of intervention and adulteration see Chapter 4, The adult role in the Play Cycle).

> **Reflective Question**
>
> How would you describe your play environment?
>
> - Which of the four best describes your play environment: Bullerby, Glasshouse, Wasteland, or Cell?
> - How does your play environment reflect the Fields of Free Action?

## The indoor and outdoor play environment, play types, and affordances

Affordances apply to both indoor and outdoor environments and to any type of play reflected in the studies of imaginative play (Laaksoharju et al., 2012), pretend play (Kyratzis, 2007), physical play (Storli & Hagen, 2010), functional play (Sandseter et al., 2022), nature play (Stordal, et al., 2015), game design (Isbister, et al., 2018), digital play (Marsh et al., 2016), and risky play (Prieske et al., 2015; Sandseter, 2009a; 2009b).

The indoor physical environment can be characterised by the following features:

- The physical space is bounded by four walls and a ceiling.
- There may or may not be windows to let in natural light.
- The space can limit the number of children able to play.
- The space may have access to electricity, which may provide light and access to digital types of play.
- The space may have access to water and heating (but not always).
- Resources usually have to be provided.
- Often the play environment will have tables and chairs.
- The space can limit the types of play.

When considering affordances and indoor play, the growth of the toy market and access to the media has influenced how children play today (Vickerius & Sandberg, 2004).

The outdoor physical environment can be characterised by the following features:

- The physical space may be bounded by walls, fences, or hedges.
- The structures in the play space may be manufactured, or natural.
- There is often constant natural light during daylight hours.
- The space may limit the number of children able to play, or can be unlimited.
- The space can promote all types of play.
- The space often has no access to electricity.
- The space may have access to water, earth, wind, and fire (but not always).
- Resources maybe provided, or naturally occurring in the environment.

The affordances outdoor environments offer for play were observed by Laaksoharju et al. (2012) in a free-time garden camp akin to a HPS. Children were observed using all their senses whilst engaged in an 'imaginative exploration and manipulation of the environment' (Laaksoharju et al., 2012, p. 201). Similarly, Storli et al. (2015) found children's contact with nature enabled them to participate and move between different self-initiated play activities (physical play, animal play, family play, hero play) incorporating the natural elements found in their play, where:

> Children are actively negotiating the affordance of nature and the natural elements, in relation to each other, to the play themes and partners involved in the play. There is a reciprocal relationship between nature and children in this ongoing play. The children are shaping the meaning of nature around them, as they utilize and respond to the negotiated affordances provided by the natural environment.
>
> (p. 31)

The natural environment offers many objects for children to play with and incorporate into their play, and it is now a common feature of Forest Schools (FS) (Ridgers et al., 2012). This can include sticks, twigs, stones, the soil, insects, and plants. The natural objects available in the play space have been used in children's play as recollected by both adult memories and their preschool children's current experiences (Vickerious & Sandberg, 2004) and relate to the concept of loose parts (Nicholson, 1971). An example of how the Play Cycle was observed in a Forest School setting is explained below:

> One example I have is Forest School where I had the experience of observing the Play Cycle not long ago which included loose parts of miscellaneous cups and hot chocolate powder placed randomly around the environment. Children would pick them up and they took them to their own play space, invited more children around, and they created a game called stars.
> (Second Year BSc Early Childhood Studies Student)

**Reflective Question**

How do the 'affordances' of your indoor and outdoor space compare?

## Loose parts

The concept of 'Loose Parts' or 'open-ended materials' (Houser et al., 2016) was first introduced by the architect Simon Nicholson in the wonderfully titled article 'How not to cheat children: The theory of loose parts' (Nicholson, 1971). Nicholson (1971) stated:

> In any environment, both the degree of inventiveness and creativity, and the possibility of discovery, are directly proportional to the number and kind of variables in it.
> (p. 30)

The number and kind of variables available in the environment are what Nicholson (1971) termed loose parts. Loose parts are objects that can be manipulated and may involve the construction, destruction, and reconstruction of the object. Loose parts can be both natural items (e.g. stones, twigs, sand, and water) or manufactured objects (e.g. tyres, rope, and boxes) (Houser et al., 2016). Loose parts are important as children need to be able to 'play with building and making things ... that satisfy one's curiosity' (Nicholson, 1971, p. 30). Gull et al. (2019) put forward this current definition of loose parts:

> Loose parts are open-ended, interactive, natural and manufactured materials that can be manipulated with limitless possibilities. Interaction with loose parts includes experimentation, exploration, and playful interactions with variables through creativity and imagination.
> (p. 48)

Since the original article was first published in 1971, the theory of loose parts has been incorporated into playwork (Gibson et al., 2017; Pereira et al, 2023), childcare (Spencer et al., 2019), early years education (Flannigan & Dietze, 2017; Smith-Gilman, 2018), and primary schools (Eichengreen et al., 2022; Mackley et al., 2022; Pereira et al., 2023). The concept of

Loose Parts Play (LLP) has evolved (Casey & Robertson, 2016; Gibson et al., 2017; Spencer et al., 2019; Xavier et al., 2023). Loose Parts Play has been defined as:

> A technique that has been developed as a means of improving the quality of the "play offer" while maximising the opportunities for child-led play and opportunities for engagement.
>
> (Gibson et al., 2017, p. 296)

Studies undertaken with Canadian preschool children, Australian upper primary school children, Dutch primary school children, and Portuguese primary school children's use of loose parts in outdoor spaces found Loose Parts Play was non-gendered, cooperative with shared goals, included a range of different play types, and involved more risk-taking (Eichengreen et al., 2022; Houser et al., 2019; Flannigan & Dietze, 2017; Mackley et al., 2022; Pereira et al., 2023; Spencer et al., 2019). This combination of creative, social, and varied play has been described as a loose-parts mindset where children can 'use open-ended materials to transform them into imaginative constructions or tales' (Smith-Gilman, 2018, p. 92) which may support physical, cognitive, social, and emotional development (Cankaya et al., 2023; Houser et al., 2016; Gibson et al., 2017). Nicholson (1971) raised an important question:

> How are variables and loose parts introduced into the world of newly born children, and what function do the variables have on cognition and perception?
>
> (p. 33)

This question can be answered by referring to the Play Menu (Hughes, 2012) which enables 'practitioners to analyse and prepare the play environment' (p. 116). The Play Menu consists of four areas: The Five Senses (touch, taste, smell, sight, and sound), Identity (who we are and who we like to be), Concepts (try and test out general ideas), and the Elements (earth, wind, fire, and water) (Hughes, 2012).

---

**Reflective Question**

How can children engage with all their senses?

How can children construct, deconstruct, and re-construct?

How can children interact with the environment, and what is available in the environment (both animate and inanimate objects)?

How can children incorporate the elements into their play?

---

These questions can be considered concerning the Play Cycle. The loose parts are in the child's external world, and they will perceive them through the five senses. This is the external perceptual cue that can stimulate the idea to play, the pre-cue. The child may send out a play cue to a specific loose part, or loose parts. Providing the child has access to the chosen loose parts (the loose parts provide the play return), a Play Cycle will form that may involve tactile touch, for example playing with sand (senses), or finding a number of cardboard boxes that are broken apart and a 'new' object is made (concepts). The loose parts may be involved in pretend play where the child is acting out a role (identity), or the child may want to make mud pies and stir the mixture with a stick (the elements). When a Play Cycle is established, play cues (and returns) continue, or what is termed as flow. Within flow, more loose parts may be incorporated into the Play Cycle, reflecting on Nicholson's (1971) definition of loose parts where the more variables (loose parts) there are, the more inventiveness and creativity take place.

An example of loose parts and the Play Menu can be demonstrated in Adventure Playgrounds. APs evolved from the idea of the 'junk playground' by the landscape architect C. Th. Sørensen (1931) where 'his invented Danish word was first translated into "waste material playground" (Newstead, 2109, p. 4), which then became known as junk playgrounds. From this initial idea in 1931, the first "junk playground", with supervision, opened at Emdrupvej (sometimes referred to as Emdrup)' (Cranwell, 2003), just outside Copenhagen in Denmark. The idea was brought over to the UK by Lady Allen of Hurtwood (1968) and the first public 'junk playground' is reported to have been set up in Camberwell, London in 1948 (Benjamin, 1961). A 'typical' AP can be described as:

> A space dedicated solely to children's play, where skilled playworkers enable and facilitate the ownership, development, and design – physically, socially and culturally – by the children playing there.
>
> (Play England (PE), 2009, p. 1)

A typical day at an AP can see children making structures using wood, hammers and nails, swinging from trees, and with adults supervising, cooking on open fires. APs enable all the senses to be stimulated, provide opportunities to access the four elements (earth, wind, water, and fire), test out concepts, and by interacting with the environment, and having control over this, develop an identity. Whilst the AP is designed for children to control, shape, and access fire, this is not possible for most other play-related spaces, for example in an ASC or HPS where they are often run on school or community premises. However, the four basic areas of the senses, identity, concepts, and elements will still apply. In addition, APs, ASCs, and HPSs provide a unique environment where children of mixed ages and abilities play together. This provides an opportunity for children to play with more able peers relating to Vygotsky's (1978) concept of the Zone of Proximal Development (ZPD) (King, 2020a).

Loose parts are important in any type of play space. Examples of how practitioners have used loose parts are shown below:

> Using loose parts in pre-school for the children to explore and develop.
> Early Years Worker

> Loose Parts play during Vacation Care by providing numerous resources and allowing the children to engage with these resources however they wish and being there to support.
> Childcare Worker

> Providing loose parts at a community play session for children to enjoy free play, knowing that playworkers are on hand should they want support.
>
> Playworker

Having a play space and the loose parts available will stimulate the idea of playing, the pre-cue. The signal to play, the play cue can be issued to another person who is an object in the environment. Providing there are sufficient loose parts, children can engage in many types of play. The types of play are considered next.

> **Reflective Question**
>
> What loose parts do you have in your play environment?
>
> How can children access these loose parts?

## Types of play

Classification of the types of play is as varied and wide-ranging as there are definitions of play. One of the most recent types of play classification is Hughes's (2002) taxonomy of 16 play types: Symbolic Play; Rough and Tumble Play; Socio-dramatic Play; Social Play; Creative Play; Communication Play; Dramatic Play; Locomotor Play; Deep Play; Exploratory Play; Fantasy Play; Imaginative Play; Mastery Play; Object Play; Role Play; and Recapitulative Play. The 16 play types were constructed from a review of the literature, however, whilst certain play types are easily observed as in rough and tumble play, others, as in recapitulation play, are open to interpretation. This aspect of openness to interpretation can be found in Functional Play (Sidhu et al., 2022).

Functional Play is often used as a 'descriptor of a category of play, of play activities in general, and as an intervention target' (Sidhu et al., 2022, p. 190). Sandseter et al.'s (2022) study of Functional Play was used as an overall category for physical and rough-and-tumble play compared to Sawyers (1994) description of Functional Play related to 'sensory stimulation from simple repetitive activities' (p. 32). Sensory stimulation leads to another common play type of sensory play.

Sensory play has been defined as 'play that provides opportunities for children and young people to use all their senses or opportunities to focus play to encourage the use of one particular sense' (Usher, 2010, p. 2). Whilst it can be argued that any type of play will engage with one or more of the senses, sensory play focuses specifically on the experience of the senses. This experience is linked to other types of play cited within the literature including sand play, musical play, and construction play. Sand play includes 'all different kinds of sand environments and materials' (Iivonen et al., 2021) and relates to the sense of touch. Musical play has been defined as a 'universal type of play that consists of activities allowing children to explore, improvise and create with sound' (Zachariou & Whitebread, 2015, p. 119) linked to hearing. Construction play involves the manipulation of materials (loose parts) where children create or construct things (Wardle, 2000). This could include blocks and another type of play, block play. Block play refers specifically to the use of unit blocks in various sizes (Askoy & Asloy, 2017).

The most commonly cited and used play types include Piaget's (1952) three types of play related to cognitive development and Parten's (1931) social play classification. Piaget classified play into three types that reflected the different stages of cognitive development: practice play (sensorimotor stage), symbolic play (pre-operational stage), and games with rules (operational stage). Parten (1932) developed a classification of social play consisting of unoccupied behaviour; onlooker behaviour; solitary; parallel; associative, and cop-operative and organised. Both Piaget's (1951) and Parten's (1931) types of play indicate a change over time. Other play types have been put forward. These include Smilansky's (1968) sociodramatic play, Sandseter's (2009a; 2009b) risky play and digital pay (Stephen & Plowman, 2014) where Marsh et al. (2016) proposed Transgressive play.

Smilansky (1968) developed criteria for sociodramatic play described as 'a form of voluntary social play activity in which preschool children participate' (p. 7). Smilansky's (1968) sociodramatic play consisted of six play elements: imitative role play; make-believe in regard to objects; make-believe with actions and situations; persistence; interaction, and verbal communication. Sandseter's (2009) risky play is defined as 'thrilling and exciting forms of play that involve a risk or physical injury' (p. 3) and consists of six categories. The six categories of risky play are Great Heights; High Speed; Dangerous Tools; Dangerous Elements; Rough and Tumble; and Disappear/Get Lost. Digital play refers to 'screen-based computer games' (Stephen & Plowman, 2014, p. 8) that can be a computer, phone, or tablet. March et al.'s (2016) study on children's digital use offered a seventeenth play type to Hughes's (2002) classification of transgressive play. Transgressive play is where 'children contest, resist and/or transgress expected norms, rules and perceived restrictions in both digital and non-digital contexts' (Marsh et al., 2016)

Whitebread et al.'s (2012) classification of the different types of play offers five variations. These are physical play (play that uses energy and movement); Object Play (play that involves an object that is used or manipulated); Symbolic Play (play that uses objects to represent, or symbolise other objects); Pretend Play (play that uses imagination and may take on different roles); and Games with Rules (play that has distinct rules, such as a sport). Whitebread et al.'s (2012) classification provides a more 'useable' play type compared to Hughes's (2002), although there is no social play type. However, children play alone, and there is no 'solo play type', and thus Whitebread et al's. (2012) use of five play types can be considered when children play alone, or with others.

The five types of play can only exist if there are adequate resources, or loose parts, within the play environment. For example, for children to engage in object or symbolic play, the environment requires 'objects' which can provide the perceptual cue to spark the pre-cue or idea to play. For physical play or games with rules such as football, there has to be an area to run, where the perceptual cue may be the space or an object such as a ball. Once a Play Cycle has formed, the type of play can be used to describe the play frame, especially when using the Play Cycle Observation Method (PCOM) where you provide a name for the play frame.

> **Reflective Question**
>
> How many of the five types of play do children engage in within the play environment you work in?
>
> Can you provide examples for each type of play you have observed?

Consideration has to be given to atypicality and types of play. For example, children diagnosed with Attention-Deficit Hyperactivity Disorder (ADHD) are less involved in cooperative play (Normand et al., 2018) but more 'adventurous' in risky behaviours (Dekkers et al., 2022) which could include more risky play.

Children diagnosed with autism are considered to engage less in symbolic, functional, imaginative, make-believe, pretend, and social types of play (Hobson et al., 2009; Honey et al., 2006; Jarrold, 2003; Kossyaki & Papoudi, 2016; Libby et al., 1998; Rutherford et al., 2007; Stahmer, 1995) which could be linked to cognitive inability (Mastrangelo, 2009). Whilst there are differences in how autistic children play compared to typically developing children, Conn (2013; 2014) states that whilst there are differences in the play experiences, children with autism do have certain play type preferences that include sensory and physical play.

The play environment will have a major influence on the types of play that can take place. Sandseter et al. (2022) found within Early Childhood Education Centres (ECEC) the most common types of play in the indoor environment were constructive and symbolic play. This was also reflected in Acer et al.'s (2016) study in a nursery school where dramatic and manipulative play were the types of play mostly observed. The commonality of constructive and manipulative play relates to the indoor space containing tables (Sandseter et al., 2022). Often the types of play children engage in are influenced by adults where resources are available, or not, for instance, where an indoor play space is 'divided' up into specific areas or zones (Çakırer & Garcia, 2010).

The play environment is an 'ecology' that comprises the space, resources, and the people within it. The interaction of the three (space, resources, people) will determine how, what, where and why children play. This chapter focused on the play environment and resources, the next two chapters will concentrate on child-led play and the adult role in the Play Cycle.

## Conclusion

This chapter considered the play environment linking to the theories of the functional cycle (von Uexküll, 1982; 2010), affordances (Gibson, 1986; Kyttä, 2004) and loose parts (Nicholson, 1971). The interaction of the play environment, the resources, and the children within the space can enable children to engage with their senses and experience different types of play (Whitebread et al. 2012).

**Further Reading**

For more on play and affordances, the following paper is suggested:

- King, P. & Sills-Jones, P. (2016). Children's Use of Public Spaces and the Role of the Adult - A Comparison of Play Ranging in the UK, and the leikkipuisto (Play Parks) in Finland. International Journal of Play, 7(1), 27-40.

# 3 The Play Cycle and child-led play

## Introduction

This chapter begins with a brief overview of the United Nations Convention on the Rights of the Child (UNCRC) with a specific focus on Article 31, the Right to Play. The chapter continues by comparing the terms child-led, child-centred, and child-directed play, and how they can have different interpretations in the context they are being used. Child-led play is the preferred term used for this chapter that leads into the concept of non-directive play. Non-directive play is a child-led process that can link to the Play Cycle. The chapter concludes with a consideration of child-led play and risk.

## The Right to Play and the United Nations Convention on the Rights of the Child

The United Nations Convention on the Rights of the Child (United Nations International Children's Emergency Fund (UNICEF, 2009) was first proposed by the Polish Government in 1978 (Quennerstedt et al., 2018) and was approved by the General Assembly on the 20 November 1989 and officially signed on the 26 January 1990 (Rico and Janot, 2021). The UNCRC consists of 54 Articles, or Rights within three broad principles, more commonly referred to as the 'three p's' of protection, participation, and provision (Campbell-Barr, 2021). The UNCRC applies to every human under the age of 18 years of age and incorporates civil, political, and social-economic rights to ensure children's basic human rights of survival and development (Campbell-Barr, 2021; McNeil, 2020; Quennerstedt et al., 2018). The UNCRC was signed by the United Kingdom (UK) Government on the 19 April 1990, ratified on the 16 December 1991, and came into force on the 15 January 1992.

The UNCRC has one specific Right concerning play, Article 31:

> States recognise the right of the child to rest and leisure, to engage in play and recreational activities appropriate to the age of the child and to participate freely in cultural life and the arts.
>
> (UNCRC 1989)

Article 31 was further enhanced by the issue of General Comment No. 17 (2013) on the importance of play in children's lives (McKendrick et al., 2018). Article 31 and the Right to Play is reflected in Government Play Policies and Strategies in Wales (Welsh Assembly Government (WAG), 2002), Republic of Ireland (RoI) (Office for Minister for Children (OMC), 2004), Northern Ireland (NI) (Office for First Minister and Deputy First Minister (OFMDFM), 2010), and Scotland (Scottish Government (SG), 2013). These policies and strategies are covered in more detail in Chapter 6.

In addition to Article 31, these government play policies and strategies also refer to the definition of play being freely chosen, intrinsically motivated, and for no external goal where children control the choice and content of their play (Garvey, 1990). How play is defined within play policies and strategies, there is often conflict concerning practice (Wood, 2022), and this is further complicated when considering child-led, child-directed, and child-led play. In whichever way, the importance of child-led play and children's rights is reflected in the following comment:

> It made me advocate child-centredness and child leadership and ownership of play as an underpinning philosophy for practice. As an important value base connected to rights, equity, resilience and wellbeing.
>
> Playworker

In the published literature there is reference to child-centred, child-directed, and child-led play. However, do these all mean the same thing? This will be considered next.

The importance of including the right to play underpins professional playwork practice

## Defining child-centred, child-directed, child-initiated, and child-led

Where the focus of play is on children, there are four concepts that appear in the published literature: child-led, child-initiated, child-centred, and child-directed. Although all focus on the child, the interpretation and application of the four concepts vary (Campbell-Barr, 2019). A child-centred approach is informed by theories of developmental psychology, cultural theories, and more recent sociological theories (Campbell-Barr, 2019; Power et al., 2019). Child-centred play has been used within education (Amani & Fussy, 2023; Cheung, 2017) where the adult often has a more active part in the content, choice, and type of play to meet a possible outcome or attainment although children may instigate their learning (Power et al., 2019). Stordal et al. (2015) found that when children were active agents and decided the rules when interacting with nature, through play 'children are free to respond differently than in an activity defined or led by an adult' (p. 35), which contributes to children's autonomy and empowerment in their play (Canning, 2007).

Whilst child-centred play places the child at the centre of play, child-directed is a more difficult term to clarify. For example, Andreasson et al., (2023) refer to the key components of child-directed play as being child-led with the focus on the play process with the child in control. However, Toub et al. (2016) includes child-directed play within guided play, where play is 'guided' by adults to a learning goal. Here, it suggests that interpreting child-directed play can be a process led by children, or a learning outcome guided by adults. Alternatively, child-directed play may be initially directed by children, or what is termed child-initiated play.

Child-initiated play has been defined as 'activities and experience are those which babies or children have indicated they want to do' (Lindon, 2010, p 2). This suggests that it is the child that will start the play, however, child-initiated play does not necessarily mean the child's intended play actually happens. In addition, child-initiated play is commonly associated with educational practice (Vaisarova & Reynolds, 2022) and learning (Maynard et al. 2013; Woods, 2017). Child-initiated play has the scope to be child-led, however, this will depend on the context of the play, how much control the child has over their play, and if the play is being met with an adult-led outcome.

Child-led play indicates more than play being initiated; it is being carried out with the child having more control. This is often associated with the term, 'free play' (Bergen, 1988) and more closely aligns with the definition of play as being 'freely chosen, intrinsically motivated for no external goal' that is referenced in play theory (Garvey, 1977), play policies and strategies (e.g. Welsh Assembly Government (WAG), 2002), and professional practice, for example, the eight Playwork Principles that underpin professional playwork practice (Playwork Principle Scrutiny Group (PPSG), 2005) as clearly indicated in Playwork Principle No. 2:

> Play is a process that is freely chosen, personally directed and intrinsically motivated. That is, children and young people determine and control the content and intent of their play, by following their own instincts, ideas and interests, in their own way for their own reasons.
>
> (p. 1)

Whilst the Playwork Principles (PPSG, 2005) relate to playwork professional practice, the focus on 'play as a process' links directly to the Play Cycle, and for children to 'follow' their own chosen play, this indicates the reason to play comes from the child, that is it being child-led. The term child-led play will be used from here onwards.

> **Reflective Question**
>
> Which do you prefer to use child-led, child-initiated, child-centred, or child-directed play?
>
> What factors influence your choice?

## The Play Cycle and child-led play

For children to take the lead in their play, this often means that the play cue is initiated by the child. Play cues can be verbal or non-verbal and the skill of the practitioner is to be able to provide a response or a play return for a Play Cycle to form. The Play Cycle and child-led play are clearly stated in the following comments:

> I see playwork as just having an understanding of what it is to be a child and being led by the child rather than using a set practice. I introduce children to different games and activities depending on what is in the environment around us but usually go by their lead.
>
> Playworker

> I would say it has helped me understand and follow the recent guidance on child-led play, children leading learning. I have been more able to step back to let children explore their own interests.
>
> Childcare Worker

Child-led play links clearly with the Play Cycle where the child, or children issue the play cue, the signal to play. However, when considering disability and atypicality, there are instances where the child can't initiate verbal or non-verbal play cues to initiate play (Smith, 2018).

Smith (2018) provides examples of where adults working with children and young people with Profound and Multiple Learning Disabilities (PMLD) had to initiate a play cue and then observe any non-verbal reactions that indicated a play return. Smith (2018) clarifies this where 'young people were not playing "with" anything but were often being played with, it was the staff that was playfully interacting' (p. 193). The importance of this is that there are times and occasions where play has to be adult-led, not for any outcome, but merely to be able to initiate a Play Cycle as reflected in the comment below:

> Generally, I wait and observe before joining in with play, giving the child the opportunity to invite me into their play if they want me to join in. However, I realise that for a majority of disabled children whom I work with, their limited communication or understanding of social skills frequently means that adults need to help them with the cueing process, reframing how they cue e.g. encouraging a child to tickle if they want to play a chasing game rather than throwing a brick at someone's head.
>
> Playworker

Autism is another aspect of atypicality to be considered. Kanner's (1943) publication noted children with 'autistic aloneness', a 'desire for sameness', and 'islets of ability'; aspects that were further developed by Wing and Gould (1979) in their 'Triad of Impairments' of social relationships, social communication, and social understanding and imagination. The Play Cycle is included in Conn's (2016) book 'Play and Friendship in Inclusive Autism Education' where play is framed within a culture that is 'patterns of behaviour and interaction that exist for and are shared amongst a group of people within a society' (p. 37). What is important here is the 'patterns of behaviour and interaction' as this will vary between typically and atypically developing children but can still be identified as play (Eilsele & Howard, 2012; Shamsudin, 2021; Willans, 2021). Another aspect to consider is how children with autism share the same play space with others where they may lack an understanding of it being a shared space with others (Conn, 2014). Focusing on the process of play and responding to a child's play cue will enable the practitioner to enter the 'cultural world' of the child, not necessarily that of the adult.

The Play Cycle and atypicality also relate to Attention-deficit Hyperactivity Disorder (ADHD). ADHD can be seen as a combination of hyperactivity, impulsiveness, and inattention (Hughes & Cooper, 2007) that may result in what appears to be a 'lack of concentration' and the 'inability to sit still'. Sturrock and Else (1998) and Sturrock (2003) proposed that children diagnosed with ADHD send out play cues at such a rapid rate that often they are not picked up, and the resulting 'inappropriate behaviour' may be down to frustration of the play cue not being recognised nor responded to, or what Rennie (2003) referred to as a 'distorted play cue' (p. 26). Sturrock and Else (1998) refer to the inability to read the play cue as 'dysplay'. This 'distorted play cue' may be interpreted by other children as negative behaviour (Normand et al., 2018). This aspect of interpreting what may be 'inappropriate behaviour' in relation to the Play Cycle has now been interpreted as 'play behaviour' (King & Newstead, 2019; 2020) where the practitioner has picked up the intended play cue.

> **Reflective Question**
>
> What differences have you observed of the types of play between typically and atypically developing children?

The Play Cycle, focusing on the process of play, enables both child-led play, and where appropriate, adult-led play concerning both typicality and atypicality. This leads to the aspect of how the Play Cycle can be used in non-directive play.

## The Play Cycle and non-directive play

Child-led play can also be referred to as a form of non-directive play used in Play Therapy (PT) (Axline, 1947) termed Non-Directive Play Therapy (NDPT). The use of non-directive play was put forward by Virginia Axline whose work was influenced by the person-centred approach of Carl Rogers (Ahuja & Saha, 2016). Non-directive play, as with other forms of PT, for example, Directive Play Therapy (DPT) is commonly used to enable children and young people to address psychosocial difficulties (Homeyer & Morrison, 2008). This can include attachment disorders (Ryan, 2004), maltreated and neglected children (Ryan, 1999), autism (Casper et al., 2021; Josefi & Ryan, 2004), movement and music (Krason & Szafraniec, 1999), anxiety (Hateli, 2021), and speech and language therapy (Cogher, 1999). Rennie (2003) referred to Axline's study with 'Dibs' (1964) as an example of a child's behaviour as a 'distorted play cue' where non-directive play is used as a therapeutic approach with children diagnosed with Autism (Kalyva, 2011).

NDPT focuses on eight basic principles developed by Axline (1947):

1. The therapist must develop a warm, friendly relationship with the child, in which good rapport is established as soon as possible.
2. The therapist accepts the child exactly as he (she) is.
3. The therapist establishes a feeling of permissiveness in the relationship so that the child feels free to express his (her) feelings completely.
4. The therapist is alert to recgonise the feelings the child is expressing and reflects those feelings back to him (her) in such a manner that he (she) gains insight into his (her) behaviour.

5  The therapist maintains a deep respect for the child's ability to solve his (her) own problems if given an opportunity to do so. The responsibility to make choices and to institute change is the child's.
6  The therapist does not attempt to direct the child's actions or conversation in any manner. The child leads the way; the therapist follows.
7  The therapist does not attempt to hurry the therapy along. It is a gradual process and is recognised as such by the therapist.
8  The therapist establishes only those limitations that are necessary to anchor the therapy to the world of reality and to make the child aware of his (her) responsibility in the relationship.

The word 'therapist' can be replaced with 'adult' (any adult working with children in a play-related context) and the word 'therapy' replaced with the word 'play'. In this respect, non-directive play relates to the Play Cycle where the child leads (child-led) the process (in this case the play process) and the adult, through responding to play cues and being involved in the Play Cycle, will develop a relationship. The aspect of the 'therapist' reflecting (or mirroring) feelings relates to the concept of the 'witness position' or 'watcher self' (Sturrock & Else, 1998; King & Temple, 2018). The 'witness position' is covered in Chapter 4, The adult role in the Play Cycle.

An example of non-directive play practice was described by King et al. (2016) when families were provided with junk modelling (loose parts) and left to create whatever structures they wanted children often led the making of the models:

> The parents, led by the children, were actively participating in discussions about design and construction. One observation they seemed to be enjoying the making of objects as much as the children with one family of four creating a six-foot totem pole.
>
> (King et al., 2016, p. 151)

Examples of when the Play Cycle has been considered indirectly with non-directive play practice is reflected in the comments below:

---

> I try to let the children take the play in the direction they wish to go. I help them by providing equipment and resources.
>
> Childcare Worker

> It has directed my practice when working in early years by allowing children to have self-directed play opportunities and to facilitate learning based on their interests.
>
> Early Years Worker

> Arguing against adults interfering or directing a child's play, especially when play is being hijacked for other functions.
>
> Playworker

Non-directive, or child-led play enables children to have the choice, volition, and autonomy (control) of their play. This can change the 'power' from adults to children, and this often raises some issues around how much control children have in their play. This is especially so when considering risk in play.

> **Reflective Question**
>
> Can you think of any examples where you may have used non-directive play in your practice?
>
> Are there examples where you could have used non-directive play in your practice?

## The Play Cycle and risk in play

When considering risk and play, the Health and Safety Executive (HSE) (2012) made this very important statement:

> Play is great for children's well-being and development. When planning and providing play opportunities, the goal is not to eliminate risk, but to weigh up the risks and benefits. No child will learn about risk if they are wrapped in cotton wool.
>
> (p. 1)

The key consideration is to 'weigh up the risks and benefits', or what is more commonly known as the 'Risk-Benefit Assessment' (R-BA) (Ball et al., 2013), and decide if there are more benefits to allowing certain types of play compared with the risk. For example, rough-and-tumble play has the risk of children getting hurt, however, there are many benefits to rough-and-tumble play. The research suggests by engaging in rough and tumble play children not only benefit from physical development but that it also contributes to the development of social skills (Scott & Panksepp, 2003) by children regulating their strength and ability (Smith and St. George, 2023). Dodd and Lester (2021) and Dodd et al. (2022) propose that children who take risks within their child-led play may be better at responding to uncertainty by developing coping mechanisms.

> **Reflective Question**
>
> How comfortable are you in allowing children to have control over the risk in their play?
>
> What examples can you recall when you have intervened and not intervened in children's play concerning risk?

When children lead the play, there will be an increase in potential 'risk' as children decide on how they want to play. The Play Cycle will therefore always have an element of 'risk', the potential to get hurt, although the adult will be present to reduce this. Children are capable of assessing risk levels in their play (Sandseter, 2009b) and risk-taking in play has been observed in children as young as two and three years old (Kleppe et al., 2017). When considering atypicality and risk in play, there may be a need for more adult 'supervision, for example, children with Autism or ADHD often lack 'safety skills' resulting in poor safety awareness with an increased risk of injury (Wiseman et al., 2017; Pardej & Mayes, 2024). However, it has been shown with adult supervision, children with autism still engage in challenges and risks in outdoor play in the same way as typically developing children (Fahy et al., 2021). This demonstrates the need to consider play and risk using the risk-benefit analysis approach for all children, where taking and managing risks in their play, particularly in outdoor environments, is a natural propensity (Brussoni et al., 2012).

> **Reflective Question**
>
> How much risk do you allow typically developing children to have in their play?
>
> How much risk do you allow atypically developing children to have in their play?

When playworkers, childcare workers, and early years workers were asked how the Play Cycle has influenced their practice, responses included risk:

> I understand now that children need to be allowed to take risk, to deal with conflict and to allow them to play in their own way.
>
> Playworker
>
> Encourage children to take risks through play and that play is children's work
>
> Childcare Worker

Supporting child-led play will involve enabling children to manage aspects of risk in their play. While there is always a safeguarding and health and safety role for adults, who in turn must work within legislative and organisational policies and procedures, the importance of children experiencing risk in their play has been acknowledged by the Health and Safety Executive (HSE) (2012). In addition, Brussoni et al. (2012) emphasise there is also a rights-based aspect to consider within Article 31 of the UNCRC.

Children's play, especially within outdoor environments, will have Play Cycles that reflect Sandseter's (2009a, 2009b) six categories of risky play: Great Heights, High Speed, Dangerous Tools, Dangerous Elements, Rough and Tumble, and Disappear/Get Lost. For example, a tree can provide the perceptual cue from the environment and a child may then stimulate the pre-cue (idea to play) to climb the tree. The play cue may be accessing the tree in order to climb it. This is reflected in the comment by an After School Club (ASC) worker below:

> One of our sites has a tree which lends itself to being climbed. I have supported the team to negotiate school rules, supervise a group of mixed-ability climbers, and defend our values and approaches to facilitate risky play by advocating the benefits.
>
> After School Club Playworker

> **Reflective Question**
>
> What are the barriers to risk and play you have experienced?
>
> How can you support child-led play to include risk?

## Conclusion

This chapter discussed the Play Cycle and the process of play that supports child-led play. Child-led play is when the child is in control and has the autonomy of their play, supported by the adult practitioner. Child-led play is discussed in relation to children's right to play as stated within Article 31 of the UNCRC. Child-led play is fundamental to non-directive play practice and can be used across any context where children play. The chapter concludes with a consideration of the need for children to manage their risk in play.

> **Further Reading**
>
> For more on Article 31 and play, the following is suggested:
>
> - Welsh Assembly Government (2002). A Play Policy for Wales. Cardiff: WAG.
>
> For more on child-led play, the following is suggested:
>
> - King, P., & Temple, S. (2018). Transactional Analysis and the Ludic Third (TALT): A Model of Functionally Fluent Reflective Play Practice, Transactional Analysis Journal, 48(3), 258-271, DOI: 10.1080/03621537.2018.1471292
>
> For more on play and risk, the following are suggested:
>
> - Health and Safety Executive (HSE) (2012). Children's Play and Leisure – Promoting a Balanced Approach. https://www.hse.gov.uk/entertainment/assets/docs/childrens-play-july-2012.pdf.
> - Ball, D., Gill, T. & Spiegel, B. (2012). Managing Risk in Play Provision: Implementation Guide. https://playsafetyforum.wordpress.com/wp-content/uploads/2015/03/managing-risk-in-play-provision.pdf.

# 4 The Play Cycle and the role of the adult

## Introduction

This chapter focuses on the adult role in supporting children's play. The chapter begins with the four hierarchical levels of Adult Intervention
Styles (AIS): play maintenance, simple involvement, medial intervention, and complex intervention. The four hierarchical levels are mapped to the Play Cycle with play maintenance and simple involvement seeing the adult in a more passive role, whereas the adult becomes more active with medial and complex intervention where they respond, and in some cases, issue play cues. Whilst the Play Cycle focuses on the process of play, the chapter describes how it can relate to, and be used within, Play-based Learning (PBL), particularly in collaborative play. The chapter concludes with how the Play Cycle and the Play Cycle Observation Method (PCOM) can be used by all play practitioners within reflective practice.

## How adults support the process of play

The adult role in the Play Cycle (King & Newstead, 2021a) is to support the process of play (King & Strurrock, 2019; King & Newstead, 2020; Sturrock & Else, 1998) and not to take over and control it for adult agendas, or what Sturrock and Else (1998) termed 'adulteration'. Adulteration is where the Play Cycle may be used for an adult-focused objective, rather than children directing the purpose of their play, for example in adult-led PBL (Pyle & Danniels, 2017).

When supporting the process of play, the adult can be involved in five of the six elements of the Play Cycle for example, by providing a play return in response to a child's play cue or in some cases, by issuing a play cue to encourage children into play. Once a Play Cycle is established, the adult may take a containing role to ensure the play frame is not interrupted which could result in the Play Cycle being interfered with or annihilated. If the adult is an active participant in the Play Cycle, they could be involved in a complex fantasy play where both the child and adult are issuing play cues in an established Play Cycle. Supporting the process of play, the role of the adult can involve four types of AIS: play maintenance; simple involvement; medial intervention; and complex intervention (Sturrock & Else, 1998; Sturrock et al, 2004).

> **Reflective Question:**
> When you are playing with children, how do you support the process of play?

36  The Play Cycle in practice

## The Play Cycle: Play maintenance, simple involvement, medial intervention, and complex intervention

Each of the four AIS are explained below in connection with the story below:

> Jane and Phil are two practitioners working in an After School Club (ASC). Jane and Phil are outside standing on the grass field watching a group of children, six girls and five boys aged between seven and nine years, in a Play Cycle playing tag (also called 'it', chase, tig, tick, and tip). Although both ensure the game does not impact other children's Play Cycles, neither are actively involved in the game nor need to intervene.
>
> During the game, one child comes over to Jane and asks them if they could get a small box and make some eye holes. Jane knows where there is a box and walks inside leaving Phil to watch the game of tag alone. The child waits with Phil for Jane to return with the box. Shortly, Jane returns and hands the child a small box with eye holes. The child thanks Jane and rushes off to the child who is currently the chaser and puts the box on their head. The game continues.
>
> As the game continues, the child who is currently the chaser (with the box on their head) rushes up to Phil, touches their arm and says, *'You're it'*. They give Phil the box and run off. Phil places the box on the top of their head and starts chasing the children. Jane watches and laughs.
>
> As Phil is chasing the group of children, one shouts out *'Look out, it's the box monster'*. Phil, listening to this, starts to growl and says, 'Whoever I catch I will eat for tea'. The children scream and try and avoid being caught by Phil. Phil continues to adopt the character of the monster, and the game of tag continues but with a new fantasy element where the children adopt different characters to avoid the monster. After five minutes of chasing, Phil touches Jane on the arm, gives them the box, and says *'You take over'*.
>
> The above story, although fictitious is believable and most of us who have worked with children in a play-based context have probably watched or been involved in a game of 'tag'. How does this play story relate to the four levels of intervention of play maintenance, simple involvement, media intervention, and complex intervention?

## Play maintenance

The Play is self-contained – no intervention is necessary; the worker observes the activity. The story begins with Jane and Phil in the AIS of play maintenance.

The group of children is in a Play Cycle of 'Tag' and the adults are passive in the Play Cycle taking on an observer role. It is not uncommon for adults in play maintenance to be observing more than one Play Cycle. For example, whilst some of the children are playing 'Tag', there could be other children playing by themselves, for example playing alone with a hoop or skipping rope, or children playing in small groups such as two children playing a game that involves them clapping hands together. The key aspect is that the adults, Jane and Phil in this example, are observing.

## The Play Cycle and the role of the adult

> Understanding the play cycle has helped me better understand the role I need to take in children's play and how to stand back and observe and effectively support children's play.
>
> Playworker

> My understanding of play and the play cycle has had an impact on my work with both children and the childcare settings I support as I am able to understand how children play and how best to observe and support them.
>
> Childcare Worker

**Reflective Question:**

Can you think of an example where you supported children's play with the Adult Intervention Style (AIS) style of play maintenance?

### *Simple involvement*

The adult acts as a resource for the play – this may be subtle, as in making a tool available for use, or more overt responding to a request from children.

The child who requested a box with eye holes for Jane showed how Jane moved from the AIS of play maintenance to simple involvement. Jane responded to the request by finding a box and making the eye holes. This has two implications for supporting the process of play. First, Jane acted as a resource responding to the request for the box. Secondly, within an established Play Cycle, children will continue to issue play cues to keep the Play Cycle going (what is termed flow), and the request for the box could be considered a play cue which if not responded to (play return) from Jane, may have resulted in a child leaving the game, although this may not have happened. Jane, whilst in simple involvement, is still passive in the Play Cycle of 'Tag'.

> Loose Parts play during Vacation Care by providing numerous resources and allowing the children to engage with these resources however they wish and being there to support.
>
> Childcare Worker

> To offer play opportunities and resources that support children's interest through to just providing the environment and loose parts and stepping back to see how children choose to use them.
>
> After School Club (ASC) Playworker

**Reflective Question:**

Can you think of an example where you supported children's play with the AIS of simple involvement?

## Medial intervention

At the request of the child, the adult becomes involved in the play – such as by offering alternatives from which the child chooses, or by initiating a game then withdrawing.

Here, the group of children playing 'Tag' suddenly includes the adult when one of the children touches Phil's arm, says 'Tag', gives them the box with eye holes, and then runs away. This is a play cue issued to Phil for the adults to become involved; Phil responded by placing the box on their head and started chasing the group of children. The adult is now an active participant in the Play Cycle as shown in the direct quotes below:

> I answered his play cue, I kicked the ball back to him. This sparked a relatively long game of "kick about".
>
> Adventure Playground Playworker
>
> I believe that I can observe the aspects of the Play Cycle and become involved only when responding to play cues.
>
> Playworker

> **Reflective Question:**
>
> Can you think of an example where you supported children's play with the AIS of medial intervention?

## Complex intervention.

There is a direct and extended overlap between playing children and the adult – the adult may need to take on a role in the play or act as a partner to the playing child.

When Phil is chasing the group of children, they issue a play cue of 'Look out, it's the box monster' and growls. The children responded by screaming and they took on different characters. The game of 'Tag' continued but developed a fantasy aspect where both the children and the adult can issue play cues within the established Play Cycle. This is complex intervention. In complex intervention, the adult is again active in the Play Cycle where a child and adult are in a deep or complex play where they are both issuing and responding to play cues. What is important here is the adult does not take over or control the play, or adulterate it, as indicated in the comment below:

> Over the years it has helped me at times to understand when I have been too enthusiastic to get caught up in a game or play type where I have gone over the boundary of facilitating play and actually taking over!
>
> Playworker
>
> I find I provide less adult led activities at my group. Instead of tables with painting, collage and junk modelling and an "Auntie" at each there might be one activity

> with an adult supporting for those who chose it, and a lot more free play going on with plenty of resources on offer for the children to create their own activities/play. I'm also less likely to try and join in a game thinking I can make it better because I'm a grown up and know how to do it properly.
>
> Childcare Worker

---

**Reflective Question:**

Can you think of an example where you supported children's play with the AIS of complex intervention?

---

For the adult practitioner, it is possible to be in more than one of these AIS levels at the same time. The practitioner is often observing other children's Play Cycles (passive role) whilst being an active participant in another one. Whether in play maintenance, simple involvement, medial intervention or complex intervention, the adult aims to keep the Play Cycles intact, within the play frame where they have a containment role (Sturrock & Else, 1998).

---

**Reflective Question:**

Can you think of a time when you were in more than one of the AIS at the same time?

---

## The Play Cycle and AIS

When containing a Play Cycle within a play frame the role of the adult is to ensure the established Play Cycle remains intact. In play maintenance, the adult's position is outside of the play frame, where they can observe and intervene if they see the Play Cycle being interrupted, or potentially going to be interrupted. For simple involvement, the adult will 'step into' the play frame, acting as a response. For both medial intervention and complex intervention, the adult is an active participant within the Play Cycle and is situated within the play frame. Although the adults are active within the Play Cycle, they still have a containment role ensuring the Play Cycles are not interrupted or taken over by the adults. The AIS of play maintenance, simple involvement, medial intervention, and complex intervention and the Play Cycle is shown in the Figure 4.1.

How the four AIS levels can support the process of play is reflected in the comment below:

> I am much more sensitive to how I affect the Play Cycle and what types of intervention are appropriate
>
> Playworker

---

**Reflective Question:**

Describe a time or situation where you have been on more than one type of AIS.

40  The Play Cycle in practice

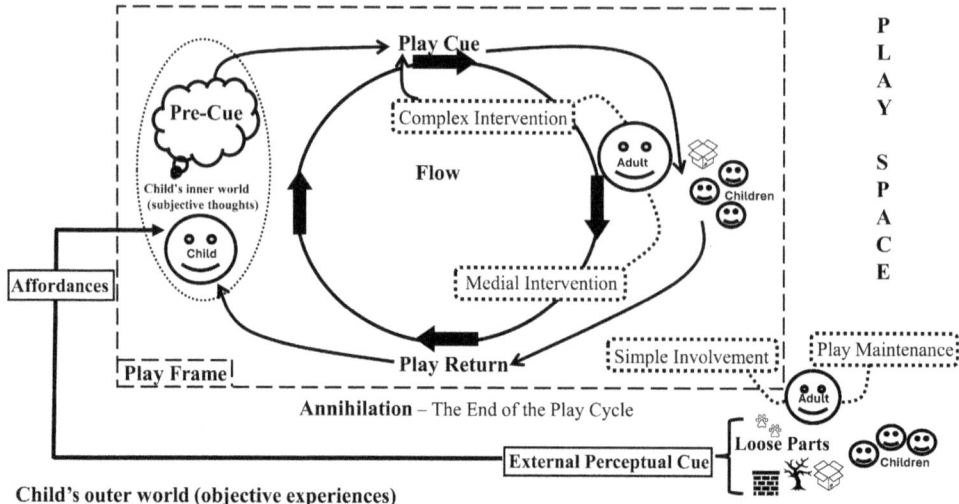

*Figure 4.1* The Play Cycle and the Adult Intervention Style

How did you manage to be in more than one AIS at the same time?

When asked how the Play Cycle supports adults in professional practice, both playworkers (King & Newstead, 2021a) and childcare workers (King & Newstead, 2022a) changed their professional practice to focus on 'play behaviour' rather than 'inappropriate' behaviour, and provided underpinning theory that reinforced current practice. However, the two studies found that whilst playworkers were more likely to support the Play Cycle in play maintenance (observer role) (King & Newstead, 2021), childcare workers, including early years practitioners, were more likely to be in medial intervention (active member in the Play Cycle) (King & Newstead, 2021). The adult role in the use of play in PBL (King, 2025) is considered further in the next section.

## The adult role in the Play Cycle and PBL

PBL has been described as a teaching approach involving playful, child-directed elements along with some degree of adult guidance and scaffolded learning objectives (Weisberg et al., 2013; Wood et al., 1976). Scaffolding relates to Vygotsky's (1978) Zone of Proximal Developed (ZPD) PBL has been defined as:

> Child-centered and focuses on children's academic, social, and emotional development, and their interests and abilities through engaging and developmentally appropriate learning experiences.
>
> (Taylor & Boyer, 2020, p. 127)

PBL uses play to meet the outcomes. For example, PBL is evident in England, in the Early Years Foundation Stage (Department for Education, 2023), in Wales within the Foundation Phase (Welsh Government (WG, 2015) which has now been replaced with the Curriculum for Wales (WG, 2020), Aistear (National Council for Curriculum and Assessment (NCCA), 2009) in the Republic of Ireland, and the Northern Ireland Curriculum Primary (Northern Ireland Curriculum, 2007). McInnes (2021) and Black (2023) provide an overview of how play

*The Play Cycle and the role of the adult* 41

is reflected within primary school curricula across the UK to support children's learning. In addition to the statutory curricula across the UK, Wales has produced a curriculum for funded non-maintained nurseries focusing on a play-based approach (WG, 2022). PBL consists of three aspects child-led, adult-led, and collaborative learning (King, 2025).

Bergen (1988) and Pyle and Danniels (2017) place PBL along a continuum. Bergen's (1998) play-based continuum places 'free play' at one end and 'work' at the other. In between, there are 'guided play', 'directed play', and 'work disguised as play'. Free play is when children have the most control over their play (and reflects the definition of play at the start of this book) and work is when the adult controls the play to an 'externally defined goal' (Bergen, 1988). Pyle and Danniels's (2017) continuum places play with 'free play' at one end and 'learning through games' at the other. In between there is 'inquiry play', 'collaborative designed play', and 'playful learning'. There is some similarity between the two continua; however, Pyle and Danniels (2017) consider the adult role in their continuum during child-directed, collaborative, and teacher-directed PBL. As highlighted in Chapter 3, The Play Cycle and child-led play, here the concept of child-directed play is used rather than child-led play (Figure 4.2).

Sturrock and Else (1998) stated that the adult role also 'intended to include parents and other adults active in playing with children' (p. 73). This would include adults being active in playing with children within PBL. The play-based continuum of child-directed and collaborative play can be linked to the four types of intervention styles: play maintenance, simple involvement, media intervention, and complex intervention.

When the adult takes a more passive role, for example in play maintenance and simple involvement, this reflects child-directed play. Here, the adult takes on a more observant role and decides whether to intervene or not. When the adult has a more active role, this occurs in medial intervention and complex intervention where a collaborative PBL approach can be used (King, 2025). This is shown in Figure 4.3:

An example of how collaborative play took place is provide below:

> The children enjoyed my involvement during the activity offering play cues.
>
> To continue the Play Cycle, I suggested the blue trays can be seats for the train.
>
> As the children took their seats, I collected tickets.
>
> Second Year BSc Early Childhood Studies Student

| | Child Directed | Collaborative | Teacher-Directed |
|---|---|---|---|
| Bergen (1988) | Free Play | Guided | Directed<br>Work Disguised as Play<br>Work |
| Pyle & Danniels (2017) | Free Play | Inquiry Play<br>Collaborative | Playful Learning<br>Learning Through Games |

*Figure 4.2* Types of play and adult role in PBL (based on Bergen, 1988; Pyle & Danniels, 2017) (Source King, 2025).

42  *The Play Cycle in practice*

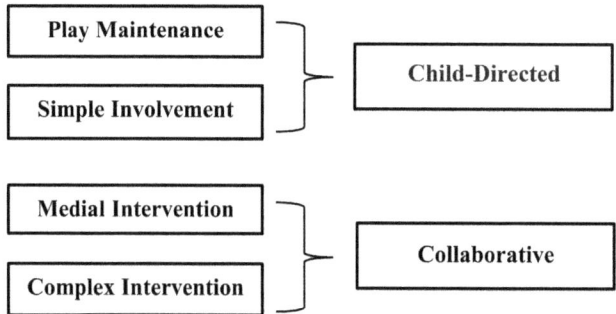

*Figure 4.3* Level of intervention and adult role in PBL (Source King, 2025)

The following scenario reflects how the levels of intervention and the PBL of child-directed and collaborative play could be applied:

> Sally has set up an activity in their pre-school where the children will be making houses out of scrap material, and this has been planned on what children should make and what resources to use *(Adult-led)*. Sally asks if any children are interested in making houses.
>
> The children see the junk material and decide to make things other than houses *(Child-Directed)*. Sally observes and reflects on what is happening as the children explore the junk scrap material *(Play Maintenance)*. One child asks Sally, 'Do you have any dressing up clothes we can use'. Sally nods and brings some over to the table *(Simple Involvement)*. The child is now playing on their own in a small area of the room.

> Another child hands Sally some junk modelling and some glue. Sally asks, 'What shall we make?' The child discusses ideas with Sally and they both agree on creating a made-up animal. The child and Sally are making the model together *(Collaborative)*. Sally makes a noise and says, 'It was not me; it was the animal'. The child laughs and they both make up noises *(medial intervention)*. Sally and the child are now in a role-playing game with the animal they have made up stories about what it does *(Complex Intervention)*. Eventually, the child has enough and goes on to play with something else.
>
> Whilst Sally is tidying up, they leave the area to put some resources away, and upon their return, three children are playing with the remaining resources *(Child-directed)*. Sally observes what they are doing *(Play Maintenance)* and asks the children 'What do you need to play with here?' *(Simple Involvement)* The children replied, 'Nothing now, we have what we need', which then enabled Sally to continue to clear away the unwanted materials.

The use of the Play Cycle within PBL is still an 'uncharted area', however, the recording of children's Play Cycles has been undertaken within pre-school provision (King et al., 2021) using the PCOM. This shows the PCOM can be used in any play-based context, including PBL.

> **Reflective Question:**
>
> If you work in early years and are involved in PBL, can you think of any examples where the Play Cycle and the four intervention styles (play maintenance, simple involvement, media intervention, and complex intervention could have been used?

When adults are involved in children's play, whether passive as in play maintenance and simple involvement, or active, within medial intervention and complex intervention, professional practice requires self-monitoring and self-evaluation. This is more commonly referred to as reflective practice.

## Reflective practice

Reflective Practice is a psychological process (Gibbs, 1988; Schön, 1983) and is now commonplace as part of professional practice in all contexts of children's services, for example, playwork (Palmer, 2002), childcare and early years (Lindon & Trodd, 2016; Reed & Canning, 2010), and childhood practice (Pollock & Stewart, 2023). An interesting interpretation of Reflective Practice comes from Edwards and Thomas (2010):

> Reflective practice is a description of how people come to be apprenticed to
>
> communities of practice, each with its own socially negotiated intentions, purposes
>
> and internal standards of judgement.
>
> (p. 411)

When breaking down this interpretation, a Community of Practice (CoP) consists of three elements: joint enterprise; mutuality; and a shared repertoire (Wenger, 1998) which involves 'shared learning, shared practice, inseparable membership, and joint exploration of ideas' (Mohajan, 2017, p. 1). Within this interpretation of reflective practice and community of practice, early years, childcare and playwork can each be considered three distinct CoPs as they have different professional standards, more commonly referred to as National Occupational Standards (NOS) (UK Commission for Employment and Skills, 2011). In addition to the NOS, there are National Minimum Standards (NMS) for any childcare or playwork provision to comply with if they have primary-school-aged children, run for more than five days a year, or more than two hours a day. Both the NOS and NMS are featured in more detail in Chapter 6.

Two aspects of reflective practice are now described: reflection-in-action and reflection-on-action.

> **Reflective Question:**
>
> What model of reflective practice do you use?

## Reflection-in-action and reflection-on-action

Palmer (2002) provides a good summary of the importance of Reflective Practice considering both Schön's (1983) reflection-in-action and Gibbs's (1988) reflection on action. Reflection-in-action 'may be directed to strategies, theories, frames, or role frames' (Schön, 1983, p. 73). Schön (1983) stated that the 'process of reflection-in-action which is central to the "art" by which practitioners sometimes deal well with situations' (p. 50) where 'knowing is *in* our action' (p. 49).

Hébert (2015) explains that Schön's (1983) reflection-in-action 'enables a practitioner to intelligently respond to a situation at hand based on an intuitive feeling that has been cultivated through experience' (p. 364) where 'reflection-in-action hinges on the experience of surprise' (Schön, 1983, p. 56). Palmer (2003) outlines Schön's (1983) reflection-in-action as a cycle: real-world experience; reflecting on what happens; making sense and using theories; and putting into action. In summary, reflection-in-action can be considered as 'thinking on your feet'.

> **Reflective Question:**
>
> Can you think of an example where you had to reflect-in-action (think on your feet) when you have been involved in children's play?

Gibbs's (1998) reflection-on-action also involves linking theory to practice. This is undertaken with practitioners 'through engaging in a cyclical sequence of activities: describing, feeling, evaluating, analysing, concluding and action planning' (p. 3). In summary, reflection-on-action can be considered as 'thinking after putting your feet up'.

> **Reflective Question:**
>
> Can you think of an example where you had to reflect-on-action (when you have put your feet up) when you have been involved in children's play?

This 'intuitive feeling' has been expressed by practitioners when asked how the Play Cycle was incorporated within their practice, where it provided a theory to underpin what they were already doing (King & Newstead, 2019).

> It enables me to promote reflective practice as a must. It is a medium to discuss adult support in a child-led process
>
> Playworker
>
> An understanding of the Play Cycle and related thinking has led me to better reflect in the moment, when I'm sufficiently focused, and to try to make alterations to my practice at that time.
>
> Playworker

*The Play Cycle and the role of the adult* 45

> It allowed me to extend my ability to reflect on play in the setting and therefore to improve the play experience for the children attending.
>
> Childcare Worker

Reflection-in-action (Schon, 1983) and Reflection-on-action (Gibbs, 1988) was considered by Dewey and Bentley (1949) in relation to observations which:

> sees man-in-action, not as something radically set over against an environing world, not yet as something merely acting "in" a world, but as action of and in the world in which the man belongs as an integral constituent.
>
> (p. 114)

## The Play Cycle and reflective practice

The Play Cycle provides an observational tool that can be used to support Reflective Practice, both reflection-on-action and reflection-in-action. Table 4.1 below provides a reflective guide and links back to topics covered in previous chapters.

*Table 4.1* Reflective guide and the Play Cycle

|  | *Reflection-in-Action* | *Reflection-on-Action* |
| --- | --- | --- |
| **Play Cue** | Who is issuing the play cues? What type of play cue is being issued? Is the same play cue being issued? Are other children aware of the play cues? Are adults aware of the play cues? Are play cues being issued to other people or objects? | Consider both the Play Cycles formed and those not formed from the play cues issued. Are play cues being interpreted as 'inappropriate behaviour?' Think about both typicality and atypicality. |
| **Play Return** | Are all the play cues being picked up? Why are some play cues not being issued a return? Are the Play Cycles long or short in duration? Are adults consistent in the play returns provided? | Consider the number of play returns that form Play Cycles. Are there barriers that are preventing play returns? Is the play environment resourced sufficiently? |
| **Play Frame** | How much space is the Play Cycle taking up? What types of play are the Play Cycles representing? | Consider how the play space may or may not permit as many types of play. Are the five types of play taking place? |
| **Annihilation** | How do the Play Cycles finish? Are the Play Cycles being ended by the children playing within them? Are other children not in the Play Cycles ending them? Are adults ending them? | Consider if Play Cycles are being interrupted or terminated by others not playing within them. Are there policies and procedures that are contributing to Play cycles being stopped? |
| **Adult Role** | How are adults supporting the Play Cycle? What types of AIS are being used? Are adults controlling or adulterating the Play Cycles? | Consider how consistent adult professional practice is when supporting Play Cycles. What is the main type of AIS being used? |

Chapter 5 outlines the PCOM which can be used to record the play cue, play return, play frame, annihilation, and the adult role which can both support professional and reflective practice. The importance of observing using the principles of the Play Cycle was demonstrated during this reflection:

> Observe the interactions, decide whether the children understood the play cue, intervene to initiate a play cue, when play cue is positively received return to observing.
>
> Second Year BSc Early Childhood Studies Student

When reflecting-in-action, observing and recording the play process of the play cue, play return, play frame, and annihilation through reflection provides the opportunity for self-awareness as you continually reflect as you practice. Sturrock (1999; 2003) referred to a practitioner's self-awareness within the Play Cycle as working within the 'witness position' or the 'watcher self'. The 'witness position' relates to both reflection-in-action and reflection-on-action, however, it is the reflection-on-action where the practitioner is aware of their own role in the Play Cycle where practitioners are aware of their subjectivity (feelings and emotions) as well as the objectivity of supporting the process of play (Sturrock, 1999; 2003; Sturrock & Else, 1998). The important aspect of reflecting in and on action within the 'witness position' is that being aware of your own subjectivity enables you to respond rather than react when supporting the process of play within the Play Cycle (King & Temple, 2018).

When reflecting-on-action the information collected from the PCOM Record Sheets can be used in individual reflective practice and supports how the team works. There is also scope for supporting and developing organisational policy and practice. The PCOM provides an observational tool to record the process of play concerning the play cue, play return, play frame, and annihilation. In addition, the AIS can be recorded. The PCOM, as well as being used to observe and record children's play, can also support reflective practice on how children play and the adult role in supporting this. The concept of play being a child-led activity supported by the adult through observations is reflected in the following comment:

> I often feel adults take charge or create rules for play when they are not necessary and the Play Cycle and playwork allows practitioners to understand the importance of child-led activities. It is also helpful for observations.
>
> Playworker

> **Reflective Question:**
>
> When you next observe children play, reflect on the process of play, for example are your play cues being picked up?

Reflect on how you are supporting the process of play within the Play Cycle for both reflection-in-action and reflection-on-action. Which type of reflection do you use most?

An adult working with children will be involved in children's play and may focus on the process of play, or play as an outcome (Howard & King, 2014). Whilst playwork focuses more on the process of play (King & Newstead, 2019) and PBL will be more outcome-focused (Pyle & Danniels, 2017), the Play Cycle and the PCOM can be used as an observational tool for reflective practice across all play-based contexts.

## Conclusion

This chapter described the four hierarchical levels of AIS: play maintenance, simple involvement, medial intervention, and complex intervention. The four intervention styles can be used when supporting the process of play where the adult may take on a more passive role in the Play Cycle (play maintenance and simple involvement) or be more actively involved (medial and complex intervention). When considering PBL, play maintenance and simple involvement can be used in child-directed play whilst medial and complex intervention can support collaborative play between children and adults. The chapter concludes with how the Play Cycle and using the PCOM can support reflective practice, both reflection-in-action and reflection-on-action. The PCOM is explained in more detail in the next chapter.

> **Further Reading**
>
> For more detailed information on adult role in the Play Cycle, the following reading is suggested:
>
> - King, P. & Newstead, S. (2021). Understanding the Adult Role in the Play Cycle—An Empirical Study. Child Care in Practice, 27(3), 212-223.
> - King, P, & Newstead, S. (2022). Childcare worker's understanding of the play cycle theory: Can a focus on "Process not Product" contribute to quality childcare experiences? Child Care in Practice, 28(2), 164-177.

# 5 The Play Cycle Observation Method (PCOM)

## Introduction

How to undertake a Play Cycle Observation using the Play Cycle Observation Method (PCOM) is explained in this chapter. The Play Cycle focuses on the process of play, and the PCOM has been trialled and developed to record the four elements of the play cycle: play cue, play return, play frame, and annihilation. The PCOM can be undertaken using video recordings of children playing (King, 2021) or in 'real time' (King et al., 2022), offering a valid and reliable method to observe and record elements of the Play Cycle

This chapter provides the tools needed to undertake a PCOM observation. When first conducting an observation using the PCOM, it is recommended to use a video of children playing so you can practice using the Record Sheets as you pause and rewind the film. The PCOM can be used in conjunction with any vocational qualification where observation of children's play is required, as well as being a useful tool for reflective practice. The PCOM is split into three aspects: Resources, Application, and Analysis. There are two resources required to undertake a Play Cycle observation: PCOM Record Sheet and the PCOM Record Sheet Table. How to undertake a PCOM observation is explained in this chapter.

## The PCOM resources

There are two resources required to undertake a Play Cycle observation: PCOM Record Sheet and the PCOM Record Sheet Table.

The PCOM Record Sheet is designed to record the information in a 'shorthand' format and covers the following elements of the Play Cycle:

- Play cue
- Play return
- Play frame
- Annihilation
- The start and finish time of an established Play Cycle (duration)
- Play cues issued in an established Play Cycle
- Type of Adult Intervention Style (AIS)

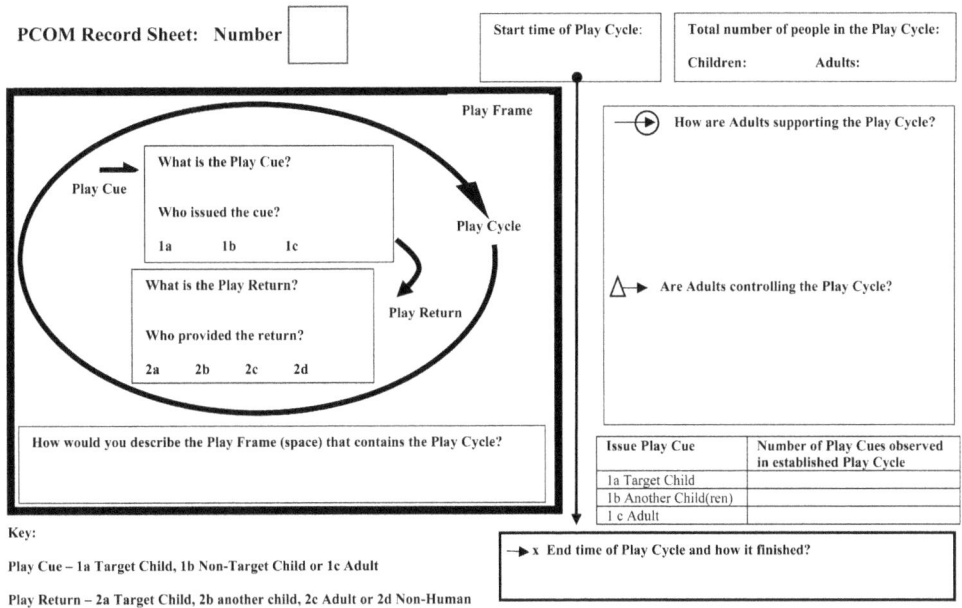

*Figure 5.1* The Play Cycle Observation Method (PCOM) Record Sheet

A new PCOM Record Sheet is completed for every Play Cycle observed during the period of the observation. Some Play Cycles may last just a few seconds whilst others may continue on for several minutes or even longer. For example, if a child is observed for ten minutes, there might be one PCOM record sheet completed containing a lengthy c. 10-minute Play Cycle, or there might be five or more Record Sheets completed in this time frame, each detailing a different play cycle which might range in duration from a few seconds to a few minutes. An example of a blank PCOM Record Sheet is shown in Figure 5.1; later on, completed examples are shown to illustrate how to fill it in:

The PCOM Record Sheet Table enables numerical data collected from all the PCOM Record Sheets completed during the observation to be collated in one place. This enables numerical analysis to be undertaken of the number of play cues issued and returned and the duration of each Play Cycle observed. A copy of the PCOM Record Sheet Table is shown in Table 5.1:

## The PCOM application

The PCOM is designed to focus on one child termed the 'Target Child' for no longer than ten minutes. There may be other children, or 'Non-Target Children' and/or 'Adults' involved in the observation; however, the focus is always on the 'Target Child'. In addition, there may be objects involved in forming Play Cycles termed 'Non-Human'. The initial play cue that could form a Play Cycle may come from the Target Child, another child, or an Adult. The play return may come from the 'Target Child', 'Non-Target Child', 'Adult', or a 'Non-Human' source. The key aspect is to record all play cues relating to the 'Target Child' (whether they are issued by them or to them), particularly as not all play cues will form or establish a Play Cycle. When using a PCOM Record Sheet, number each one sequentially.

50  The Play Cycle in practice

Table 5.1 The Play Cycle Observation Method (PCOM) Record Sheet Table

| Record Sheet | Play Cue Issued | | | | Play Return | | | | Time | Play Cues in Established Play Cycles | | | |
|---|---|---|---|---|---|---|---|---|---|---|---|---|---|
| | Column 1 | Column 2 | Column 3 | | Column 4 | | | | Column 5 | Column 6 | Column 7 | Column 8 | |
| | TC | N-TC | A | | TC | N-TC | A | N-H | | TC | N-TC | A | |
| PCOM 1 | | | | | | | | | | | | | |
| PCOM 2 | | | | | | | | | | | | | |
| PCOM 3 | | | | | | | | | | | | | |
| PCOM 4 | | | | | | | | | | | | | |
| PCOM 5 | | | | | | | | | | | | | |
| PCOM 6 | | | | | | | | | | | | | |
| PCOM 7 | | | | | | | | | | | | | |
| PCOM 8 | | | | | | | | | | | | | |
| PCOM 9 | | | | | | | | | | | | | |
| PCOM 10 | | | | | | | | | | | | | |
| PCOM 11 | | | | | | | | | | | | | |
| PCOM 12 | | | | | | | | | | | | | |
| PCOM 13 | | | | | | | | | | | | | |
| PCOM 14 | | | | | | | | | | | | | |
| PCOM 15 | | | | | | | | | | | | | |
| PCOM 16 | | | | | | | | | | | | | |
| PCOM 17 | | | | | | | | | | | | | |
| PCOM 18 | | | | | | | | | | | | | |
| PCOM 19 | | | | | | | | | | | | | |
| PCOM 20 | | | | | | | | | | | | | |
| Add Up Each Column Total | TC Play Cues | N-TC Play Cues | A Play Cues | | Play Cycles Formed (Add All the Returns Together) | | | | Add All Times Together | TC Play Cues | N-TC Play Cues | A Play Cues | |
| Average | | | | | | | | | | | | | |

Key: TC = Target Child; N-TC = Non-Target Child; A = Adult; N-H = Non-Human (e.g., object)

*The Play Cycle Observation Method (PCOM)* 51

The following seven-step process explains how to use the PCOM Record Sheet when undertaking an observation. When observing and recording the play cue (step 1), there may not be a play return (step 2), and if so, then only the play cue is recorded. When this happens, start a new PCOM Record Sheet and start at step 1 again. Remember, PCOM Record Sheets that only record an initial play cue are important to keep when collating all the PCOM Record Sheets into the PCOM Record Sheet Table.

1. Focusing on the 'Target child', begin to observe any play cue ➡ and briefly write down what the play cue is. The play cue could be issued by the Target Child, a 'Non-target child', or an 'Adult'. For example, the Target Child may kick a ball to a Non-Target Child, or the other way around where a Non-Target Child kicks a ball to the Target Child. The next step is to code who issues the cue. In the example provided if the Target Child issued the play cue, circle 1a on the PCOM Record Sheet. If a Non-Target Child issued the cue, circle 1b. If an adult issued the play cue, circle 1c. Note down the start time of the first play cue and briefly write down what the play cue was.
2. If the play cue is given a response, a play return ↙ is produced. If the play return is from the Target Child, circle 2a. If the play return is from a Non-Target Child, circle 2b. If the play return is from an Adult, circle 2c. If the play return is from a Non-Human source (e.g., object in the environment, animal, etc.), circle 2d. Briefly write down what the play return was. Remember, not all play cues will get a play return. If this is observed, and no play return is produced, write down 'no response' and start a new PCOM Record Sheet.
3. The combination of the play cue and play return will result in a Play Cycle ⟲ being formed. The Play Cycle will be contained in the play frame.

   ▢ The play frame may be a bounded physical space (e.g., a sand pit) or a non-bounded psychological space (e.g., a word game). Describe the play frame: the physical or psychological space where the Play Cycle is taking place (this could be the type of play, the game or activity, or the space where the Play Cycle is taking place).
4. Once the Play Cycle has been established, play cues do not stop. Continue to record the play cues issued by the Target Child, Non-Target Child, and/or Adult in the established Play Cycle. This can be undertaken using a scoring system where every time a play cue is observed within the established play cycle, a stroke (/) can be placed in the 'Issue Play Cue' section of the PCOM Record Sheet.
5. Throughout the Play Cycle, observe and record the AIS and make notes on the PCOM Record Sheet. Are the adults supporting the Play Cycle for example, are the adults taking an observer role or do they provide resources to help keep the Play Cycle going? Or are the —⊕ adults controlling the Play Cycle where △➡adults may be demonstrating adulteration.
6. When the Play Cycle comes to an end, this is annihilation ➤ x. Record the time the Play Cycle finishes ↡. Write down how the Play Cycle finishes on the PCOM Record

52   *The Play Cycle in practice*

> Sheet and who finished it: the Target Child, Non-Target Child, or Adult. Annihilation may be because of a Non-Human reason. Record the total number of children and adults in the Play Cycle.
> 
> 7   Once a Play Cycle has finished, start using a new PCOM Record Sheet and record when a new play cue is observed. Again, if there is no response to the play cue, then 'no response' is written on the PCOM Record Sheet as no Play Cycle is formed. If there is a play return, record this as a new Play Cycle is established. Record the start time and continue to record any play cues in the established Play Cycle as before.

## Example of a PCOM observation using a recorded video of children playing

The example of the PCOM used video recording of children playing. The video is briefly described below:

> The video was a recording of four children and one adult playing in a preschool in America. The play involved the children playing with beads and other objects, including funnels, beakers, and scoops on a raised large tray. The four children were situated at each corner of the raised tray, two were sitting, and the other two were standing. The PCOM undertaken focused on one child (Target Child). The recording was a total of 3 minutes and 8 seconds in duration.

The three-minute PCOM observation resulted in three PCOM Record Sheets being used. The start and finish times were obtained from the video time stamp. For example, when the first play cue was observed, the time indicated on the time stamp was used to record the start of a potential Play Cycle. If the play cue had a play return, this was recorded and the video was watched to record any play cues within the established Play Cycle. When the Play Cycle was annihilated (finished), the time indicated on the time stamp was used. The length (duration) of the Play Cycle was worked out by the difference between the two times recorded (play cue and annihilation). A brief description is provided which relates to the narrative data analysis explained further on.

The PCOM Record Sheet number 1 has a play cue recorded at 25 seconds from the Target Child (1a) (Figure 5.2). The play cue of a verbal request was picked up by an Adult (2c) who provided a verbal play return and gave up the chair they were sitting on which the child used. A Play Cycle was established as the child started to play with beads in the space given up by the 'Adult'. The 'Adult' supported the formation of the Play Cycle by giving up their chair which is Simple Involvement (acting as a resource). The play frame was a corner of the large tray that contained beads. The Play Cycle was annihilated at 2 minutes and 36 seconds by a Non-Target Child issuing a play cue. This Play Cycle lasted 2 minutes and 11 seconds and only involved the 'Target child'. The play cue issued to the Target Child started a new PCOM Record Sheet.

The PCOM Record Sheet number 2 had a non-verbal play cue from a Non-Target Child (1b) issued at 2 minutes and 36 seconds (from the video recording time-stamp) where they

The Play Cycle Observation Method (PCOM) 53

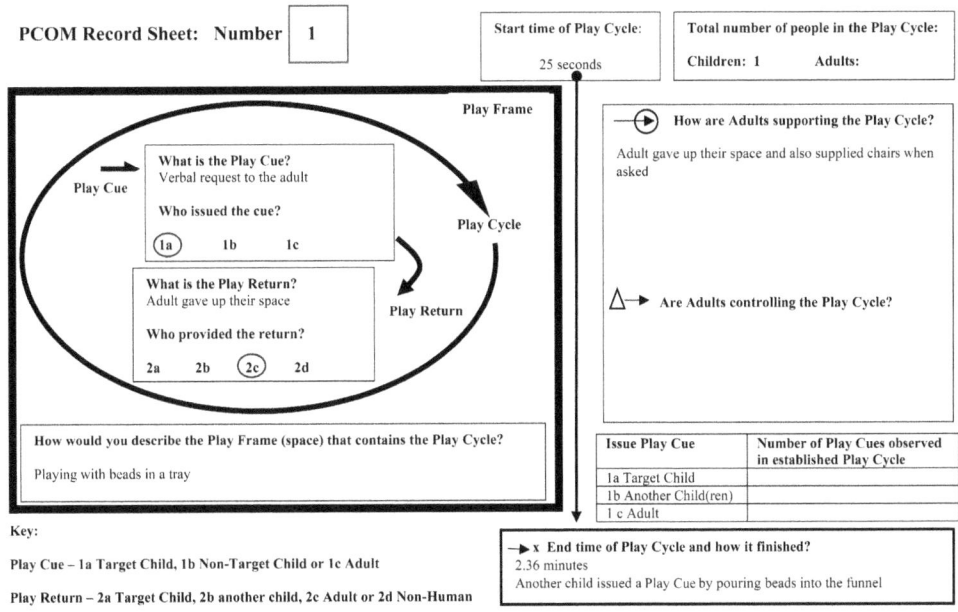

Figure 5.2 PCOM Record Sheet Example 1

poured beads into a funnel being held by the Target Child (Figure 5.3). The Target Child provided a non-verbal play return (2a) by holding the funnel for more beads to be poured in. An established Play Cycle formed. There were no play cues from either the Target or the Non-Target Child in the established Play Cycle. The play frame was still the bead tray but now increased in size as two children were in this Play Cycle. The Non-Target child issued a play

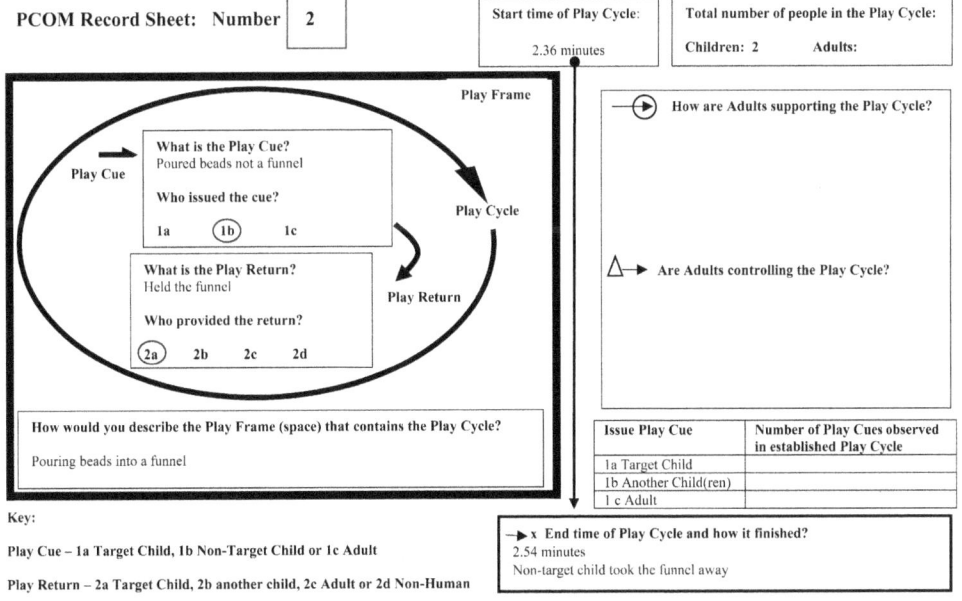

Figure 5.3 PCOM Record Sheet Example 2

## 54  The Play Cycle in practice

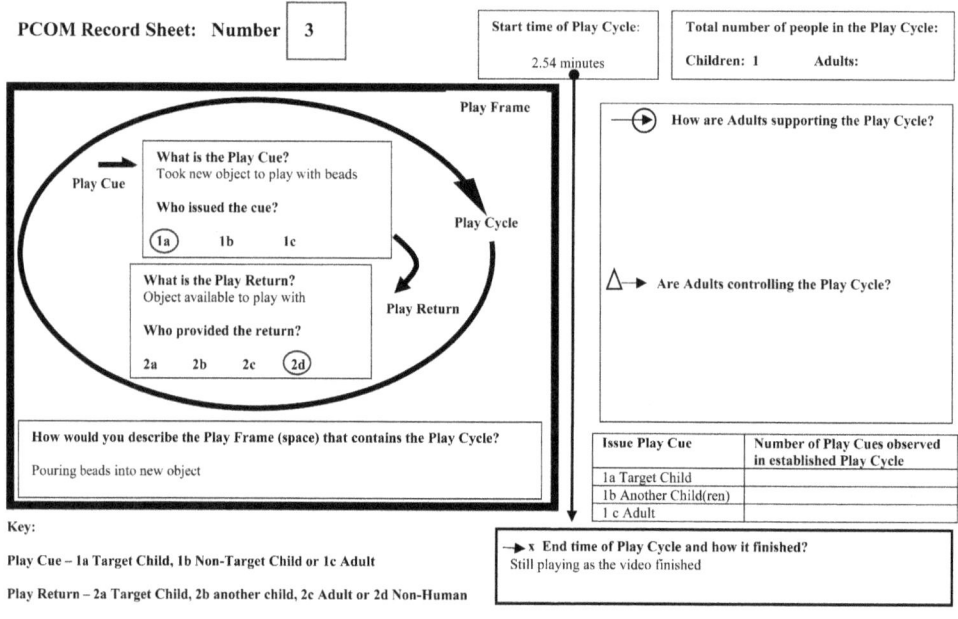

Figure 5.4  PCOM Record Sheet Example 3

cue to the 'Target Child' in the Established Play Cycle by holding the funnel. The Non-Target Child annihilated the Play Cycle when they started to use the funnel on their own. This was at 2 minutes and 54 seconds, and the length of the Play Cycle was 18 seconds. No Adults participated in the Play Cycle.

With the Non-Target Child using the funnel, the Target Child issued a play cue (1a) to use a different object to play with the beads at 2 minutes and 57 seconds. The play return was Non-Human (2d) and the Target Child continued to play on their own. The play frame returned to being the corner of the bead tray as only one child was now in a Play Cycle. The video recording ended with both children engaged in solitary play at 3 minutes 8 seconds.

This example has shown how to record information on the PCOM Record Sheets (Figure 5.4). Once you have completed your PCOM observation, the data collected from the PCOM Record Sheets can be transferred into a PCOM Record Sheet Table.

## Transferring the information to the PCOM Record Sheet Table

The PCOM Record Sheets provide data about who issues play cues both prior to, and within, established Play Cycles, the number of play returns that form a Play Cycle, and when the established Play Cycle ends (annihilates). The PCOM Record Sheet Table enables all the data from each of the PCOM Record Sheets to be put in one place.

When you undertake a PCOM observation, the number of PCOM Record Sheets used will vary. Table 5.2 records up to 20 PCOM Record Sheets, you may record less than 20, but if you have used more PCOM Record Sheets, enlarge the table. Enter each individual PCOM Record Sheet in the PCOM Record Sheet Table. Remember, not every Play Cue issued will have a return; therefore, not all the columns will have data to enter. It is important to enter

The Play Cycle Observation Method (PCOM) 55

Table 5.2 The Play Cycle Observation Method (PCOM) Record Sheet Example 1

| Record Sheet | Play Cue Issued | | | Play Return | | | | Time | Play Cues in Established Play Cycles | | |
|---|---|---|---|---|---|---|---|---|---|---|---|
| | Column 1 | Column 2 | Column 3 | Column 4 | | | | Column 5 | Column 6 | Column 7 | Column 8 |
| | TC | N-TC | A | TC | N-TC | A | N-H | | TC | N-TC | A |
| PCOM 1 | ✓ | | | | | ✓ | | 2 minutes 11 seconds | | | |
| PCOM 2 | | ✓ | | ✓ | | | | 18 seconds | | | |
| PCOM 3 | ✓ | | | | | | ✓ | 11 seconds | | ✓ | |
| PCOM 4 | | | | | | | | | | | |
| PCOM 5 | | | | | | | | | | | |
| PCOM 6 | | | | | | | | | | | |
| PCOM 7 | | | | | | | | | | | |
| PCOM 8 | | | | | | | | | | | |
| PCOM 9 | | | | | | | | | | | |
| PCOM 10 | | | | | | | | | | | |
| PCOM 11 | | | | | | | | | | | |
| PCOM 12 | | | | | | | | | | | |
| PCOM 13 | | | | | | | | | | | |
| PCOM 14 | | | | | | | | | | | |
| PCOM 15 | | | | | | | | | | | |
| PCOM 16 | | | | | | | | | | | |
| PCOM 17 | | | | | | | | | | | |
| PCOM 18 | | | | | | | | | | | |
| PCOM 19 | | | | | | | | | | | |
| PCOM 20 | | | | | | | | | | | |
| Add Up Each Column Total | TC Play Cues | N-TC Play Cues | A Play Cues | Play Cycles Formed (Add All the Returns Together) | | | | Add All Times Together | TC Play Cues | N-TC Play Cues | A Play Cues |
| Average | | | | | | | | | | | |

Key: TC = Target Child; N-TC = Non-Target Child; A = Adult; N-H = Non-Human (e.g., object)

all PCOM Record Sheets into the PCOM Record Sheet Table even when only a play cue has been recorded (so only Columns 1, 2, or 3 will have data entered).

The PCOM Record Sheet Table enables each PCOM Record Sheet to be entered individually into eight columns. When there is only a play cue and no return, depending on who issued the play cue, only Columns 1, 2, or 3 will have data being entered. If the play cue has a play return, Column 4 will then have data entered. If during the established Play Cycle there are play cues observed, there may be data to enter for Columns 6, 7, and 8. See steps 1-8 below.

1. Put a tick or mark in Column 1 if the Target Child initiates the play cue.
2. Put a tick or mark in Column 2 if the Non-Target Child initiates the play cue.
3. Put a tick or mark in Column 3 if an Adult initiates the play cue.
4. If the play cue has a response, put a tick or mark in Column 4 next to who provided the play return (this could be the Target Child, Non-Target Child, Adult, or a Non-Human source).
5. Column 5 is the length of the Play Cycle, and this is worked out from the time of the initial play cue to annihilation (remember, if no play return is given, then no Play Cycle forms).
6. In Column 6, write the number of play cues the Target Child issued in an established Play Cycle.
7. In Column 7, write the number of play cues the Non-Target Child issued in an established Play Cycle.
8. In Column 8, write the number of play cues the Adult issued in an established Play Cycle.

The data from the three PCOM Record Sheets have been entered into the following PCOM Record Sheet Table. In this example, all the play cues had a play return. Remember, if there is a play cue but no play return, still enter the play cue data for the PCOM Record Sheet.

## The role of the adult in the PCOM

The role of the adult provides narrative data that can be linked to the four hierarchal levels of support. The narrative data may indicate if the adult is taking over and controlling the Play Cycle (adulteration), or is supporting the Play Cycle, and how. As the adult role in the Play Cycle is observed, the following questions are considered:

- Is the adult taking on an observational role (Play Maintenance)?
- Is the adult providing a resource but not an active participant in the Play Cycle (Simple Intervention)?
- Is the Adult cued in by the Target Child and is an active participant in the play cycle (Medial Intervention)?
- Are the Adult and Target Child both issuing play cues and play returns in a play cycle (Complex Intervention)?

## The Play Cycle Observation Method (PCOM)

- Is the adult controlling and directing the play rather than supporting the Play Cycle (adulteration)?
- Was the adult involved in the ending of the Play Cycle (adulteration)?

It is more than likely that the adult may show one or more levels of intervention in one Play Cycle during the observation, both within the same Play Cycle and between different ones.

The PCOM Record Sheet provides details of the types of play cues and play returns, and can show information about whether they were verbal or non-verbal cues and whether resources were used or not. The play frame description can provide some information on different types of play. When the Play Cycle is annihilated, how this happened can vary concerning who, what, when, and why it finished. All this provides more narrative analysis data.

## The PCOM analysis

Once you have imputed the data into the PCOM Record Sheet Table, the following analysis can be undertaken for initial play cues, established play cycles, initiated play cues within established play cycles, length of play cycles, and how the play cycle finishes (annihilates and what type of AIS was observed). The PCOM analysis can be considered in four aspects: play cues issued, play returns, duration, and play cues in established Play Cycles.

## Play cue issued ➡

From the total number of PCOM observation sheets, the number of play cues issued by the 'Target Child', 'Non-Target Child', or 'Adult' can be calculated. This analysis will provide details of who and how often play cues are initiated:

1. Add up the total number of initial play cues issued by the Target Child (column 1).
2. Add up the total number of initial play cues issued by Non-Target Children (column 2).
3. Add up the total number of initial play cues issued by Adults (column 3).

Once you have added up each column, it is possible to work out some averages to compare how may play cues are issued between the Target Child, Non-Target Child, and the Adult:

1. Divide the total number of initial play cues issued by the Target Child by the number of play cues issued in total (whether issued by the Target child, Non-Target Child, or Adult) and multiply by 100 (column 1/column 1 + column 2 + column 3 × 100) to calculate the percentage of play cues issued by the 'Target Child'.
2. Divide the total number of initial play cues issued by the Non-Target Child by the number of play cues issued in total (whether issued by the Target child, Non-Target child, or Adult) and multiply by 100 (column 2/column 1 + column 2 + column 3 × 100) to calculate the percentage of play cues issued by the Non-Target Child.

> 3  Divide the total number of initial play cues issued by the Adult by the number of play cues issued in total (whether issued by the Target Child, Non-Target Child, or Adult) and multiply by 100 (column 3/column 1 + column 2 + column 3 × 100) to calculate the percentage of play cues issued by the Adult.

This part of the analysis relates to the number of play returns observed in relation to the number of play cues issued. The play return may be from a Target Child, Non-Target Child, Adult, or a Non-Human source, and will provide the number of play cycles established.

## Play return

This part of the analysis relates to the number of play returns observed concerning the number of play cues issued. The play return may be from a Target Child, 'Non-Target Child, 'Adult', or a Non-Human source, and will provide the number of play cycles established.

> 1  Add up the number of play returns by combining those from the Target Child, Non-Target Child, Adult, and Non-Human (column 4). This will give you the number of Play Cycles formed.

The number of play cycles formed in relation to the total number of play cues issued can be calculated as a combined 'Target', 'Non-Target', and 'Adult'.

> 2  Divide the total number of established play cycles by the total number of play cues (Target Child + Non-Target Child + Adult) and multiply by 100 (column 4/column 1 + column 2 + column 3 × 100) to calculate the percentage of established play cycles in relation to total play cues initiated.

There number of Play Cycles formed in relation to the number of play cues issued by the Target Child, Non-Target Child, or Adult can also be calculated:

> 3  Divide the total number of established Play Cycles by the total number of play cues issued by the Target Child and multiply by 100 (column 4/column 1 × 100) to calculate the percentage of established Play Cycles in relation to total play cues initiated by the Target Child.
> 4  Divide the total number of established play cycles by the total number of play cues issued by the Non-Target Child and multiply by 100 (column 4/column 2 × 100) to calculate the percentage of established play cycles in relation to total play cues initiated by the Non-Target Child.
> 5  Divide the total number of established play cycles by the total number of play cues issued by the Adult and multiply by 100 (column 4/column 3 × 100) to calculate the percentage of established play cycles in relation to total play cues initiated by the Adult.

## Time

By recording the time when the play cues are issued and the time when the Play Cycle is annihilated, it is possible to calculate the duration (total time) of all the Play Cycles combined. From this point, the average duration of a Play Cycle can be found.

> 1. Add up the total number of seconds for each Play Cycle (column 5).
> 2. Divide the total number of seconds by the total number of Play Cycles established and multiply by 100 (column 5/column 4 × 100) to calculate the average Play Cycle duration.

Remember, if watching a video, the start time is the number of seconds/minutes from the time stamp. If doing it in real-time, the start time will be zero seconds.

The duration of each Play Cycle may vary, and this could relate to whether the Play Cycles only involve a solitary person (Target Child) or may involve others (Non-Target and/or Adult).

## Play cues initiated in established Play Cycles

Once a Play Cycle is established, play cues and returns continue; this relates to the aspect of flow. Although the initial play cue may be from the Target Child, Non-Target Child, or Adult, within the established Play Cycle, the issuing of play cues may also be from different people who are in the Play Cycle. This analysis will provide details of who and how often play cues are initiated within established Play Cycles:

> 1. Add up the total number of initial play cues issued by the Target Child in the established Play Cycle (column 6).
> 2. Add up the total number of initial play cues issued by Non-Target Child in the established Play Cycle (column 7).
> 3. Add up the total number of initial play cues issued by the Adult in the established Play Cycle (column 8).

This analysis will provide a comparative average of which and how often play cues are initiated in established Play Cycles:

> 1. For the established Play Cycle, divide the total number of initial play cues issued by the 'Target Child' by the total number from the Target Child, Non-Target Child, and the Adult and multiply by 100 (column 6/column 6 + column 7 + column 8 × 100) to calculate the percentage of play cues issued by the Target Child in the established Play Cycle.
> 2. For the established Play Cycle, divide the total number of initial play cues issued by the Non-Target Child by the total number of Target Child, Non-Target Child, and the Adult and multiply by 100 (column 7/column 6 + column 7 + column 8 × 100) to calculate the percentage of play cues issued by the Non-Target Child in established Play Cycles.

> 3  For the established Play Cycle, divide the total number of initial play cues issued by the 'Adult' by the total number of Target Child, Non-Target Child, and the Adult and multiply by 100 (column 8/column 6 + column 7 + column 8 × 100) to calculate the percentage of play cues issued by Adult in established Play Cycles.

The data analysis from the three PCOM Record Sheets is shown in Table 5.3:

Further analysis can be undertaken from the PCOM Record Sheet Table. The total frequencies (total numbers) and calculated percentages (averages) from the PCOM Record Sheet Table can be calculated as shown in the Table 5.4:

The PCOM Frequency and Percentage Table (developed by Mugford, 2023, unpublished) enables further analysis. For example, you might only have undertaken a single PCOM observation with a Target Child, or you might have undertaken more than one observation on the same Target Child. You may have undertaken a single PCOM observation with several different Target Children. The PCOM Frequency and Percentage Table enables you to compare the frequency and percentage of play cues, play returns, Play Cycles, length of Play Cycles, and the play cues issued within established Play Cycles, both within the same Target Child or between different Target Children.

## Interpreting the data

The PCOM provides both quantitative and qualitative data focusing on the process of play. The PCOM provides quantitative data on the number of play cues, both before and within established Play Cycles, the number of play returns to form Play Cycles, and how long they last. This data enables a comparison with the 'Target Child' to both the 'Non-Target Child' and 'Adult' involved in the PCOM observation. From the analysis undertaken, here are some questions you can consider when you interpret the data collected.

> - How successful was the Target Child in issuing play cues to form Play Cycles compared to the Non-Target Child or the Adult?
> - How successful was the Target Child in issuing play cues in established Play Cycles compared to the Non-Target Child and Adult?
> - How many of the total play cues formed Play Cycles?
> - Why might the play cues from the Target Child not be picked up by the Non-Target Child or Adult?
> - Why may the play cues from the 'Non-Target Child' or 'Adult' not be picked up by the 'Target Child'?
> - Are play cues being interpreted as play cues by children?
> - Who was most dominant in forming Play Cycles in the established Play Cycles?
> - What is the duration of the Play Cycles (how long do they last)?
> - Is the play environment well enough resourced to support short and long Play Cycles?
> - Are there policies and practice in place that could be preventing Play Cycles being established?

The Play Cycle Observation Method (PCOM)   61

Table 5.3 The Play Cycle Observation Method (PCOM) Record Sheet Example 2

| Record Sheet | Play Cue Issued | | | | Play Return | | | Time | Play Cues in Established Play Cycles | | |
|---|---|---|---|---|---|---|---|---|---|---|---|
| | Column 1 | Column 2 | Column 3 | | Column 4 | | | Column 5 | Column 6 | Column 7 | Column 8 |
| | TC | N-TC | A | TC | N-TC | A | N-H | | TC | N-TC | A |
| PCOM 1 | ✓ | | | | | | | 2 min 11 secs | | | |
| PCOM 2 | | ✓ | | ✓ | | | | 18 secs | | ✓ | |
| PCOM 3 | ✓ | | | | | | ✓ | 11 secs | | | |
| PCOM 4 | | | | | | | | | | | |
| PCOM 5 | | | | | | | | | | | |
| PCOM 6 | | | | | | | | | | | |
| PCOM 7 | | | | | | | | | | | |
| PCOM 8 | | | | | | | | | | | |
| PCOM 9 | | | | | | | | | | | |
| PCOM 10 | | | | | | | | | | | |
| PCOM 11 | | | | | | | | | | | |
| PCOM 12 | | | | | | | | | | | |
| PCOM 13 | | | | | | | | | | | |
| PCOM 14 | | | | | | | | | | | |
| PCOM 15 | | | | | | | | | | | |
| PCOM 16 | | | | | | | | | | | |
| PCOM 17 | | | | | | | | | | | |
| PCOM 18 | | | | | | | | | | | |
| PCOM 19 | | | | | | | | | | | |
| PCOM 20 | | | | | | | | | | | |
| Add Up Each Column | TC lay Cues | N-TC Play Cues | A Play Cues | Play Cycles Formed (Add All the Returns Together) | | | | Add All Times Together | TC Play Cues | N-TC Play Cues | A Play Cues |
| Total | 2 | 1 | 0 | 1 TC + 1 A + 1 N-H = 3 | | | | 2 minutes 40 seconds | 0 | 1 | 0 |
| Average | 67% | 33% | 0% | 100% | | | | | 0% | 100% | 0% |

Key: TC = Target Child; N-TC = Non-Target Child; A = Adult; N-H = Non-Human (e.g., object)

Table 5.4 The PCOM Frequency and Percentage Table

| Observation number: | | Frequency | Percentage |
|---|---|---|---|
| Play cues issued by | Target Child | | |
| | Non-Target Child | | |
| | Adult | | |
| Play returns given | Target Child | | |
| | Non-Target Child | | |
| | Adult | | |
| | Non-Human | | |
| Play cycle formed | | | |
| Average length of play cycles | | | |
| Play cues in established play cycle | Target Child | | |
| | Non-Target Child | | |
| | Adult | | |

The answers to these questions can indicate how passive or dominant the 'Target Child' is before initiating a Play Cycle, or within an established Play Cycle, as well as the number of people involved. The amount and duration of Play Cycles can be assessed where the 'Target Child' may be involved in a short number of Play Cycles lasting minutes or a long number of Play Cycles lasting mere seconds.

More qualitative data can be derived from the PCOM about the types of play frames being described and how the Play Cycles are annihilated. Qualitative data include the type of play cue (verbal or non-verbal), the type and nature of the play frame, and how the Adult either supports or controls the play cycle. The type of AIS can be assessed where the 'Adult' takes a more passive role as an observer in Play Maintenance or resource within Simple Involvement, or a more active role in the Play Cycle as in Medial Intervention or Complex Intervention. The active role can be considered concerning how much control the Adult appears to have over the Play Cycle, and whether they are involved in adulteration. The three PCOM Record Sheet examples discussed earlier provide this type of narrative data.

The PCOM was used to observe and record the process of play by a PhD Student at Griffin University, Queensland, Australia, who remarked:

> I have been investigating the Play Cycle process and the use of the PCOM as an observation method in Family Day Care settings. My findings have shown how important it is for educators to be able to evaluate their role within a Play Cycle and to be able to observe the children's ways of starting a play cue.
>
> (Kerry Smith, PhD Student)

## Undertaking the PCOM in real-time

The PCOM can be used in real-time; however, unlike when using a video, there is only one chance to observe and record any play cues or play returns. To undertake the PCOM when observing children, you will need a timer, and any play cue issued will be recorded as zero seconds and the timer will start. If there is a play return, and a Play Cycle is established, the timer will continue until the Play Cycle is annihilated. Once the Play Cycle is annihilated, the timer is stopped, and you will have the duration of the Play Cycle which you write down on the PCOM Record Sheet. Remember, record any play cues that are observed in the established Play Cycle.

When undertaking the PCOM, try and situate yourself where you can observe the Target Child but not get in the way or disturb their play. You may be issued a play cue. You may become a passive or active part of the Target Child's Play Cycle. If this occurs, still record this as part of the PCOM observation. The PCOM observation in real-time does not need to be any longer than ten minutes.

## The PCOM and other play observational tools

The PCOM records four of the six elements that make up the process of play within the Play Cycle. The PCOM can be used as a stand-alone observation method or in conjunction with other play observation tools. For example, the PCOM could be used in conjunction with Canning's (2010) observational tool around play and empowerment, Rubin's (1989) sociability type of play, and Lifter et al.'s (2022) Developmental Play Assessment (DPA). Whilst these three examples focus on a particular aspect through play observations (empowerment, sociability, and development, respectively), the PCOM with a focus on the process of play can be used in conjunction with these and other play-related observation tools.

## Conclusion

The PCOM is an observation tool that focuses on the process of play. The recording of the play cue, play return, and duration of Play Cycles provides quantitative data for analysis. The hierarchal level of intervention, the play frame, annihilation, and types of play cues and returns can provide qualitative type data for analysis. The PCOM can be used to watch children play through video or in 'real-time'. The PCOM is an observational tool that records the process of play and can therefore be used to observe and record the process of play for analysis. The PCOM can also be used for reflective practice.

> **Further Reading**
>
> For more information on the background and the two pilot studies for the PCOM, please refer to:
>
> - King, P. (2020). The Play Cycle Observation Method (PCOM): A Pilot Study. International Journal of Playwork Practice, 1(1), Article 1. https://doi.org/10.25035/ijpp.01.01.02.
> - King, P., Atkins, L., & Burr, B. (2021). Piloting the Play Cycle Observation Method in 'real time': Recording Children's Play Cycles in Pre-School Provision. Journal of Early Childhood Research, 19(3), 298-308. https://doi.org/10.1177/1476718X20969851.

> **Video Resource**
>
> The Play Cycle Observation Method (PCOM) is explained concisely in the following videos:
>
> - https://youtu.be/UWNs3L6BEXw?si=8P84ynMg4Ni41WA-
> - https://youtu.be/NCJ5YBLdWWk?si=L7ixHFt6OgLxXid_ (subtitled).

# 6 The Play Cycle in policy and practice

## Introduction

This chapter considers how the Play Cycle can be used to support practitioners who work within childcare and playwork provision who are undertaking vocational qualifications to meet the National Occupational Standards (NOS). The Play Cycle can also support practitioners who work with or are responsible for childcare and playwork provisions that are registered and regulated to meet the play components of the National Minimal Standards (NMS). The chapter also considers how play, more specifically Article 31 of the United Nations Convention on the Rights of the Child (UNCRC) (United National International Children's Emergency Fund (UNICEF), 2017), is reflected in Government policies and strategies published by the Welsh, Scottish, Northern Ireland, and the Republic of Ireland Governments which support children's freely chosen and self-directed play.

## Government play policies and strategies and the UNCRC

In Chapter 3 (The Play Cycle and Child-Led Play), the UNCRC (UNICEF, 2019) was outlined with specific reference to Article 31, the right to play. As a reminder, Article 31 States:

> States recognise the right of the child to rest and leisure, to engage in play and recreational activities appropriate to the age of the child and to participate freely in cultural life and the arts.
>
> (UNICEF, 2019)

The understanding and importance of Article 31 and the right to play have been highlighted by the publication of General Comment 17 (United Nations (UN), 2013). The UNCRC and Article 31 underpin and have shaped play policies and play strategies in Wales (Welsh Assembly Government, 2002; 2006), Northern Ireland (Office of the First Minister and Deputy First Minister (OFMDFM), 2008; 2011), and Scotland (Scottish Government, 2013a). England does not currently have a play policy or play strategy as these were scrapped as a result of a change in the UK Government in 2010 and the introduction of austerity measures (Voce, 2015).

Wales was the first country in the world to publish a government play policy 'A Play Policy for Wales' (WAG, 2002). This was followed by the publication of the 'Play Policy

Implementation Plan' (PPIP) (WAG, 2006), otherwise known as the play strategy. The play policy stresses the importance of 'The child's free choice of their play is a critical factor in enriching their learning and contributing to their well-being and development' (WAG, 2002, p. 2). Both the Play Policy for Wales (2002) and the Play Policy Implementation Plan (2006) are underpinned by the UNCRC:

> The Welsh Assembly Government, in seeking to ensure the full implementation of Article 31 of the Convention, intends that this statement should contribute to creating an environment that fosters children's play and underpins a national strategy for providing for children's play needs (Welsh Assembly Government.
>
> (WAG), 2002, p. 3)

In addition to being the first country to have a play policy and play strategy, Wales was also the first country to have a statutory duty for play under The Family and Children Measures (Wales) 2010 (legislation.gov, 2010a). Within The Family and Children Measures (Wales) 2010, each local authority has to undertake a Play Sufficiency Assessment (PSA) every three years (WG, 2014).

The second country to publish a play policy was the Republic of Ireland (RoI) where:

> The issue of play is being addressed by the Republic of Ireland (RoI) Government to meet commitments made in the UN Convention on the Rights of the Child (1989).
>
> (NCO, 2004, p. 10)

The Republic of Ireland (RoI) published its national play policy in 2004 with the main aim of 'creating better play opportunities for children' (National Children's Office (NCO), 2004, p. 8). The play policy set out to 'ensure that children's play needs are met through the development of a child-friendly environment' (Office of the Minister for Children (OMC), 2004, p. 9). In 2007, The Republic of Ireland published 'Teenspace: National Recreation Policy for Young People (OMC, 2007). One objective of this young people's recreation (play) policy was to 'Ensure that the recreational needs of young people are met through the development of youth-friendly and safe environments' (OMC, 2007, p. 3).

Scotland published their play strategy in June 2013 within four domains (Scottish Government (SG), 2013a): in the home; at nursery and school; in the community and positive support for play. The Scottish play strategy stresses that 'We should enable all children and young people to realise their right to play' (SG, 2013a, p.15). This was followed by the publication of the Play Strategy Action Plan (SG, 2013b). The Scottish Play Strategy has undergone two progress reviews since its publication (Play Scotland & Elsley, 2020, p. 2021) and commissioned? a literature review of children and young people's views of play to inform a revision of the 2013 Play Strategy for Scotland (Nugent, 2024).

Scotland has also placed a statutory duty for the 32 local authorities in Scotland to undertake a PSA as part of their strategic planning within the Planning (Scotland) Act 2019 (legislation.gov. 2019). Under The Planning (Scotland) Act 2019, a PSA must be undertaken by planning authorities within local authorities for evidence reports. Scotland Play Policy (SG, 2013) is also underpinned by the UNCRC:

> To improve play experiences for all children and addresses our obligations in relation to children's right to play as set out in the United Nations Convention on the Rights of the Child. It is a Vision we can work towards together.
>
> (Scottish Government (SG), 2013, p. 6).

Scotland has now published the UNCRC (Incorporation) (Scotland) Act 2024 that enshrines the UNCRC into Scottish law.

Northern Ireland (NI) published their 'Play and Leisure Statement for Northern Ireland' (Office of the First Minister and Deputy First Minister (OFMDFM), 2008) with a vision to 'recognise, respect and resource play is to recognise, respect and value childhood' (p. 3). Following the 'Play and Leisure Statement', the 'Play and Leisure Plan' (OFMDFM, 2011) was published in 2011. The UNCRC features in Northern Ireland's 'Play and Leisure Statement':

> The ten-year strategy has its foundation in the United Nations Convention on the Rights of the Child, which was ratified by the UK Government in December 1991, and which recognises the importance of play and leisure activities for the child (Office of First Minister and Deputy First Minister.
>
> (OFMDFM), 2008, p. 4)

The importance of the UNCRC and the prominent inclusion within Government play policies and strategies will support play practice across all contexts where children have the right to play. This right to play could be in their leisure time, within a childcare facility, in hospitals, homes; basically anywhere where children play. The Play Cycle, with the focus on the process of play and the adult supporting this, can be applied to support UNCRC Article 31, the right to play, and the different UK play policies and strategies published individually by the Welsh, Scottish, Northern Ireland, and Republic of Ireland's governments.

Whilst Wales, Scotland, the Republic of Ireland, and Northern Ireland have governments that have published play policies and strategies, there is no legal duty for playwork, childcare, or early years providers to adhere to them, although it is encouraged.

---

**Reflective Question**

How does your professional practice reflect children's right to play?

---

The following comments show how children's rights of play relate to anywhere children play, whether in playwork, childcare, or an educational setting:

> I use it a lot when trying to advocate for the freedom of children to choose their own behaviour wherever they find themselves. I work with a lot of schools and childcare settings where they are largely focussed on education or care outcomes
>
> Playworker

> I always remind myself that children have their right to choose what to play, they can choose to play and not to play. And we will not be the ones to force the children but to respect their choice.
>
> Playworker

The Play Cycle provides the opportunity for practitioners to use a rights-based approach to their practice. Children having control over the content and choice of their play, with the adult supporting the process of play provides the basis and framework for reflecting a child's right to play as stated in Article 31 of the UNCRC (UNICEF, 1989) and the various government play policies and strategies.

Whilst there is no legal requirement for governmental play policies and strategies, there are legal requirements for practitioners to meet concerning their practice and vocational qualifications. These will be considered next when considering the NMS and NOS.

## The Children Act and regulation and inspection of childcare settings

At the same time as the UNCRC was passed (UNICEF, 2019), the legal requirement for childcare and playwork settings and organisations to be registered and inspected also changed as a result of the Children Act 1989 (legislation.gov.uk 1989). The Children Act 1989 was 'to make provision with respect to fostering, child minding and day care' (p. 1). The underlying principle of the Children Act 1989 is:

> The child's welfare is paramount and must be considered in the broad context of his physical, emotional and educational needs, his age, sex and background and the capacity of those who look after him to care adequately.
>
> (Packman & Jordan, 1991, p. 323)

The introduction of the Children Act 1989, and the subsequent legislation of the Care Standards Act 2000 (UK Parliament, 2000), the Children Act 2004 (legislation.gov.uk, 2004), and the Childcare Act 2006 (legislation.gov.uk, 2006) has direct relevance to childcare within Part XA of the Act 'Childminding and Day Care for Children'. Childcare and playwork provisions or settings attended by children aged under eight years may be required to register with their relevant inspection body. The Children Act 1989 chiefly applies to England and Wales. Scotland produced their own legislation when it published the Children (Scotland) Act 1995 (legislation.gov.uk, 1995a) that provided legislation on the care of children in Scotland and the Children (Northern Ireland) Order 1995 (legislation.gov.uk, 1995b) is the principal statute governing the care, upbringing and protection of children in Northern Ireland.

The current registration and inspection of childcare settings varies across the four UK nations of Wales, England, Scotland, and Northern Ireland. In England, the registration and inspection of childcare settings is undertaken by the Office for Standards in Education (Ofsted) and there are three types of registration:

- Early Years Register - children aged from 31 August following their fifth birthday who attend for more than two hours per day.

- General Childcare Register: Compulsory for children from 1 September following their fifth birthday up to the age of eight who attend for more than two hours per day.
- General Childcare Register: Voluntary Part for children aged eight years or over, or provision that is otherwise exempt from registration.

Childcare settings who register with the Early Years Register are settings who provide services for children who have not started primary school and have to meet both the learning and development requirements and the safeguarding and welfare requirements of the Early Years Foundation Stage (EYFS) (Department for Education (DfE) 2023). For those providers who provide care for children who have started the reception class year, they are exempt from delivery of the learning and development requirements and are afforded some relaxation of the regulations, for example ratios, staff qualifications, and space requirements. If a childcare setting is run as part of the school, separate registration is not required, and they can operate under their existing registration as a school.

In Wales, the legislation set out in the Children Act 1989 and Care Standards Act 2000 was incorporated into the Child Minding and Day Care (Wales) Regulations 2002 and registration is nowincorporated into Part 2 of the Children and Families (Wales) Measure 2010 and the Regulation of Child Minding and Day Care (Wales) Order 2016. In Wales, registered childcare provisions and settings are inspected against the 'National Minimum Standards (NMS) for Regulated Childcare for children up to the age of 12 years' which involves the total care for children aged up to 12 years for more than two hours in any day,for more than five days a year (Welsh Government, 2023). Whilst registration, regulation, and inspection in England went to Ofsted (DoE, 2023), in Wales this is the responsibility of the Care Inspectorate Wales (CIW). The CIW Inspection Framework falls within four headings: Wellbeing; Care and Development; Environment and Leadership and Management (CIW, 2021).

In Scotland, registration and inspection fall within the Care Inspectorate (CI) as set out in the Public Services Reform (Scotland) Act 2010 (legislation.gov, 2010). The NMS in Scotland falls within the 'Health and Social Care Standards: My support, my life' (Scottish Government (SG), 2017). The standards in Scotland can be applied:

> .. to a diverse range of services from child-minding and daycare for children in their early years, housing support and care at home for adults, to hospitals, clinics and care homes.
> (SG, 2017, p. 4)

The standards are based on five headings: Dignity and respect; Compassion; Be included; Responsive care and support; and Wellbeing (SG, 2017). Wellbeing refers to participating in recreation activities, playing outdoors and exploring the natural environment. Scotland has revised the Scottish Social Services Code of Practice to promote the rights and interests of individuals (Scottish Social Services Council (SSSC), 2024).

In Northern Ireland, there are 16 Standards within the 'Childminding and Day Care for Children Under Age 12: Minimum Standards (Department of Health (DoH), 2018) as set out in the 'Children (NI) Order 1995 (legislation.gov, 1995b). Any childcare provision or setting with children under 12 years of age must be registered with one of the five local Health and Social Care Trusts (HSCT) as set out in the 'Children (NI) Order 1995 and the Children (NI)

Order 1995: Guidance and Regulations Volume 2 Family Support, Child Minding, and Day Care' (Department of Health and Social Services (DoH) and the Office of Law Reform, 2018). The 16 Standards are grouped under four headings: Quality of Care; Quality of Staffing, Management and Leadership; Quality of the Physical Environment, and Quality of Monitoring and Evaluation (DoH, 2018). Childcare settings now have to register when they have children up to 12 years of age attending and when they run for two hours a day or more.

The statutory requirement for registration and inspection of childcare and early years in the Republic of Ireland falls under the Child Care Act 1991 (Early Years Services) Regulations 2016 (gov.ie, 2016). Registration and Inspection is undertaken by TULSA Early Years Inspectorate (TULSA, 2024) under the Child and Family Agency Act 2013 (Irish Statute Book (ISB), 2013). The TULSA Quality and Regulatory Framework (TULSA Child and Family Agency, 2018) is grouped under four areas of Governance, Health Welfare and Development of the Child, Safety, and Premises and Facilities.

## The Play Cycle and the NMS

Within the Registration and Inspection for Wales, Scotland, and Northern Ireland, there are specific 'standards' that relate to play. Whilst play is often linked to learning, well-being, or development, the use of the Play Cycle and the focus on the process of play can support practitioners in meeting the relevant play-specific standard. The specific play-related standards for each country, called the NMS are provided below.

In Wales, the NMS consists of 25 Standards with one Standard focusing on play. This is Standard 7: Opportunities for play and learning which has the following stated outcome:

> Children have a range of experiences, including freely chosen, unstructured and self-directed play, that contribute to their emotional, physical, social, intellectual, language and creative development.
>
> (WG, 2023, p. 25)

The childcare provision or setting is responsible for meeting children's individual needs, resourcing the play environment, providing indoor and outdoor play opportunities, and observing how children play (WG, 2023).

There are five standards in Scotland's 'Health and Social Care Standards: My support, my life'. Each standard encompasses five headings: Dignity and respect; Compassion; Being included; Responsive care and support; and Wellbeing (SG, 2017). Within the heading of Wellbeing, there is specific guidance for children to experience different types of play: freely chosen play and play outdoors to include the natural environment (SG, 2017).

In Northern Ireland, there are 16 Standards within the 'Childminding and Day Care for Children Under Age 12: Minimum Standards (Department of Health (DoH), 2018) where under the heading of 'Quality of Care' Standard 2. Care. Development and Play states:

> Children's wellbeing is promoted and their care, developmental and play needs are met. A broad range of play and other activities is provided to develop children's physical, social, emotional & intellectual abilities.
>
> (DoH, 2018, p.12)

This includes both indoor and outdoor play spaces, and both natural and manufactured resources, which are also referenced within Standard 8. Equality with 'Quality of Care'. Section 3, 'Quality of the Physical Environment' under Standard 13: Equipment refers to play resources, and Standard 14: Physical Environment includes both the indoor and outdoor play environment.

In The Republic of Ireland (RoI), the 'Quality and Regulatory Framework' (TUSLA, 2018) consists of 21 Regulations linked to the Child Care Act 1991 (Early Years Services) Regulations 2016. Within this legislation Regulation 20: Facilities for Rest and Play under the area of Health, Welfare and Development of the Child requires that 'The management and relevant staff are aware of their roles and responsibilities concerning the facilities required for play both indoors and out' (TUSLA, 2018, p. 45). In addition, there has to be a specific 'Policy on Outdoor Play' (Tusla, 2018) where 'Relevant staff are aware of their roles and responsibilities in implementing the service's policy on outdoor play if such play is provided to children attending the service' (p. 49). The Quality and Regulatory Framework makes clear reference to different types of play including risky play and the need to have resources to 'encourage both active physical play and quiet play activities' (TUSLA 2018, p. 40).

> **Reflective Question**
>
> When comparing the specific standards for play, how similar or different are they between the four UK nations?
>
> How do these play-related standards relate to the respective countries' play policies and strategies?

The application of the Play Cycle will meet the play-related standards particularly where freely chosen play is the preferred definition of play across all types of settings. This is reflected in the comment below:

> I am currently working with preschoolers in a play and childcare centre. The play cycle forms the basis for a lot of my practice there. Though many of the children are pre-verbal, relationships and communication develop quickly between adult and child when the adult demonstrates an understanding of play cues given by the child, and how to respond to these.
>
> Playwork Trainer

The NMS relates to the registration and inspection of any child-related setting. In any setting that is registered and inspected, there is a requirement for enough of the staff to be qualified to show professional competency. Professional competency relates to being observed and assessed in practice and to demonstrating knowledge, skills, and understanding. There are several vocational courses that are underpinned by NOS. There are also courses available that are not linked to the NOS, for example, Customised Qualifications such as the NCFE PARS playwork courses (Common Threads, 2024). Whilst these courses are not linked to the NOS, this book can be used to support these qualifications.

## The Play Cycle and the NOS

NOS underpins professional practice and applies to the whole of the UK. NOS are defined as:

> Statements of the standards of performance individuals must achieve to be competent when carrying out functions in the workplace, together with specifications of the underpinning knowledge and understanding.
>
> (Carroll & Boutall, 2011, p. 4)

NOS are developed through Sector Skills Councils (SSCs) and other Standard Setting Organisations (SSOs) in partnership with employers, key partners, and individuals (UK Commission for Employment and Skills, 2011). NOS provides the performance criteria and the knowledge and understanding which are expected within a vocational qualification.

There is a range of vocational qualifications from Level 2 to Level 4 in England, Level 2 to Level 5 in Wales, and Northern Ireland, and the equivalent of Level 6 to Level 9 in Scotland. In England, the main qualifications childcare workers currently study are those that are linked to the Early Years Foundation Stage Framework (EYFSF) (Department for Education (DfE), 2023a; 2023b). The EYFSF (2023) applies to all group and school-based early years providers in England s well as settings that provide Wraparound Care (WAC), an After School Club (ASC) or Holiday Playscheme (HPS). The main qualifications are the Level 2 Diploma for the Early Years Practitioner (England) (C&G, 2019a) and the Level 3 Early Years Practitioner (Early Years Educator) and Early Years and Childcare (City & Guilds, 2021). The NCFE CACHE also offers the Level 2 Diploma for the Early Years Practitioner (NCFE CACHE, 2023a) and the Level 3 Diploma for the Early Years Workforce (Early Years Educator).

Depending on the vocational course being undertaken, the course content may be directly related to the NOS, referred to the NOS, or although an accredited course, do not link in with the NOS. Where they are directly linked, the vocational course consists of a set of standards, each standard having a distinct code. Each standard is made up of an outcome, performance criteria, knowledge and understanding. Where the vocation course is referred to as the NOS, the set of standards is referred to as Units. Each Unit consists of a code, learning outcome, assessment criteria, and an overall aim.

Social Care Wales (SCW) is the Sector Skills Council for early years and childcare in Wales responsible for overseeing the necessary qualifications to work within these two areas (Social Care Wales, 2018). In Wales, two main childcare qualifications can be undertaken. The first is the childcare qualification at Level 3 Children's Care, Learning, and Development (SCW, 2023) available for practitioners and students studying for practitioner status as part of their degree. This qualification is mapped to the NOS. The second qualification is the City & Guilds (C&G)/Welsh Joint Education Committee (WJEC) Children's Care, Play, Learning & Development, which is only specific to Wales and is not mapped to the NOS (C&G/WJEC, 2020a) Children's Care, Play, Learning & Development can be studied at Level 2 for Core (C&G/WJEC, 2020b), Practice (C&G/WJEC, 2020c), and Practice & Theory (C&G/WJEC, 2020d). This qualification can also be studied at Level 3 Practice (C&G/WJEC, 2020e) and Practice & Theory (C&G/WFEC, 2020f) and at Level 4 (C&G/WJEC, 2021a; 2021b). Those undertaking the qualification can progress to Level 5 Leadership and Manage of Children Care, Play, Learning, and Development: Practice (C&G/WJEC, 2024).

*The Play Cycle in policy and practice* 73

In Scotland, the Scottish Qualifications Authority (SQA) is available at Level 6 and Level 7 Social Services (Children and Young People) (Scottish Vocational Qualification (SVQ), 2021a; 2021b) on the Scottish Credit and Qualifications Framework (SCQF). There is also the Higher National Certificate (HNC) in Childhood Practice (Scottish Qualifications Authority (SQA), 2018). The SQA also has Playwork vocational qualifications at Levels 6, 7, and 9 (SQA, 2024).

In Northern Ireland, there is the Level 2 City & Guilds Diploma in Children's Care Learning and Development (Northern Ireland) (City & Guilds, 2019b) and the Level 3 Diploma in Children's Care Learning and Development (Northern Ireland) (City & Guilds, 2020). The NCFE CACHE also provides a Level 2 Diploma for Children's Care, Learning and Development (Northern Ireland) (NCFE CACHE, 2022) and a Level 3 Diploma for Children's Care, Learning and Development (NCFE CAC|HE, 2023). In addition, both Northern Ireland and Wales have the NCFE/CACHE Level 2 and Level 3 qualifications.

Playwork qualifications across the UK can be undertaken through the NCFE. This includes the Level 2 Diploma (NCFE CACHE, 2023d), the Level 3 Certificate and the Level 3 Diploma (NCFE CACHE, 2023e). There is also the Level 3 Award Transition to Playwork (NCFE CACHE, 2024) In Wales only, there is also the Level 5 Diploma (NCFE CACHE, 2023f).

In Wales, there are other playwork qualifications Agored Level 2 Award in Playwork Practice, Agored Level 2 Certificate in Playwork Principles in Practice (P3), and the Agored Level 3 Diploma in Playwork Principles into Practice (P3) (Play Wales, 2022) linked to the NOS. Outside of Wales, Common Thread provides the NCFE Customised Qualification playwork qualification PARS Playwork Practice at Level 2 to Level 4 which are not linked to the NOS.

Play features throughout many of the Units and Standards across the playwork, childcare, and early years NOS. When considering the Play Cycle, the following questions which formed the basis of this book also relate to the Performance Criteria and the Knowledge, Skills and Understanding which have to be demonstrated by the candidate undertaking the vocational qualification:

- How is the play space set up for Play Cycles to take place?
- What resources and activities are available to promote different types of play?
- How is child-led/child-centred/child-directed play being facilitated?
- What Adult Intervention Style (AIS) is being used to support Play Cycles?
- How can the theory of the Play Cycle support other theories?
- How can the Play Cycle be used to undertake observations of play?
- How can the Play Cycle be used within reflective practice?

The specific Standards for the vocational qualifications directly related to the NOS have a set of Performance Criteria (P) linked to Knowledge, Skills, and Understanding (K), both allocated a number (for example P1 or K1). For vocational qualifications not directly linked to the NOS, the Standards are referred to as Units, the Performance Criteria as Learning Outcomes, and the Knowledge, Skills and Understanding as Aims. Mapping the Performance Criteria/Learning Outcomes and the Knowledge, Skills and Understanding/Aims of the Play Cycle and the Play Cycle Observation Method (PCOM) has been grouped into seven key areas of Play Environment; Resources and Activities; Child-centred; AIS; Theory; Observations, and Reflective Practice and link to the the seven questions above (and in Chapter 1). Table 6.3

Table 6.3 Current vocational courses

| | Level 2 (Level 6 Scotland) | Level 3 (Level 7 Scotland) | Level 4 (Level 9 Scotland) |
|---|---|---|---|
| Across the UK | NCFE Level 2 Diploma in Playwork | NCFE Level 3 Award in Transition to Playwork<br>NCFE Level 3 Certificate in Understanding Playwork<br>NCFE Level 3 Diploma in Playwork | |
| England | City & Guilds Diploma for the Early Years Practitioner<br>NCFE CACHE Diploma for the Early Years Practitioner | City and Guilds Early Years Practitioner (Early Years Educator)<br>NCFE CACHE Diploma for the Early Years Workforce (Early Years Educator) | |
| Wales | City & Guilds/WJEC Children's Care, Play, Learning and Development: Core<br>City & Guilds/WJEC Level 2 Children's Care, Play, Learning and Development: Practice<br>City & Guilds/WJEC Level 2 Children's Care, Play, Learning and Development: Practice and Theory<br>Agored Level 2 Award in Playwork Practice (Qualifies for Holiday Playschemes or in any Playwork setting if held with a relevant level 2 or above)<br>Agored Level 2 Certificate in Playwork Principles into Practice (P3) | Social Care Wales Children's Care, Learning, and Development<br>City & Guilds/WJEC Level 3 Children's Care, Play, Learning and Development: Practice<br>City & Guilds/WJEC Level 3 Children's Care, Play, Learning and Development: Practice and Theory<br>Agored Level 3 Diploma in Playwork Principles into Practice (P3) | City & Guilds/WJEC Level 4 Preparing for Leadership and Management in Children's Care, Play, Learning and Development<br>City & Guilds/WJEC. Level 4 Professional Practice in Children's Care, Play, Learning and Development.<br>City and Guilds Level 5 Leadership and Management of Children's Care, Play, Learning and Development: Practice<br>NCFE Level 5 Advanced Diploma in Playwork |
| Northern Ireland | City & Guilds Diploma in Children's Care Learning and Development (Northern Ireland)<br>NCFE CACHE Diploma for Children's Care, Learning and Development (Northern Ireland) | City & Guilds Diploma in Children's Care Learning and Development (Northern Ireland)<br>NCFE CACHE Diploma for Children's Care, Learning and Development (Northern Ireland) | |
| Scotland | SCQF The Social Services (Child and Young People)<br>SCQF Childhood Practice<br>SQV in Playwork | SCQF The Social Services (Children and Young People) including Modern Apprenticeships<br>SQV in Playwork | HNC Childhood Practice<br>SQV in Playwork |

shows the current vocational courses across the United Kingdom where the Play Cycle and PCOM can be used.

## The Play Cycle – Performance Criteria/Learning Outcomes and Knowledge, Skills, and Understanding/Aims

The Play Cycle and the PCOM can be used to meet specific play-related Performance Criteria (P); Learning Outcomes (LO), and Knowledge, Skills, and Understanding/Aims (K) in the following key areas: Play Environment; Resources and Activities; Child-Centred; AIS; Theory; Observations; and Reflective Practice. These key areas do not just apply to the Standards/Units specifically related to play. The Play Cycle and PCOM can also apply to non-play Standards/Units where play, or more accurately the process of play, can relate to topic areas such as communication, relationships, and reflective practice. For example, using the Play Cycle or PCOM can also support performance criteria and the knowledge and understanding concentring the play environment that has been set up.

Where these keywords relate to specific play Standards/Units, the Play Cycle and PCOM can provide both the practical application and the theory. The adult supporting the process of play can support children's right to how, when, and where they want to play. By responding to play cues, or facilitating the play space (for example, providing resources), children's choice of play can be supported. In addition to supporting Article 31, the right to play, supporting children's choice of their play relates to Article 12 (children's right of choice) and Article 13 (children's right to express their choice).

The Play Cycle and PCOM can also be used within non-specific play Standards/Units, for example, holistic development, inclusion, additional learning or support needs, positive behaviour, supporting families, creativity, communication, and evaluating the play environment. The inclusion of the Play Cycle and the PCOM can provide supporting evidence where play is used within the examples provided, for example, the Play Cycle will involve communication through play cues and play returns. Communication within families can use play as a method of engaging with their children where parents and carers are encouraged to pick up children's play cues. Through play, and the Play Cycle, relationships between children and adults can form, building trust and confidence.

The important aspect of the Play Cycle and the PCOM is that it can be used as evidence for both play and non-play-related Standards and Units relevant to the person's chosen vocational course. Table 6.4 below links the key areas (Play Environment, Resources and Activities, Child-Centred, AIS, Theory, Observations, and Reflective Practice) to Keywords that appear within the Performance Criteria/Learning Outcomes, and the Knowledge, Skills, and Understanding/Aims. These are both linked to the Play Cycle and PCOM.

## Higher education and practitioner status

Many Higher Education Early Childhood Studies undergraduate courses have a placement component that provides 'Practitioner Status' upon completing the course. The 'Practitioner Status' is linked to the NOS performance criteria and knowledge and understanding. An example of this is the BSc Early Childhood Studies with Practitioner Status at Swansea University. Students

76  The Play Cycle in practice

Table 6.4 Key areas, keywords, and the Play Cycle

| Key Areas Around Play | Keywords with the Performance Criteria (P)/ Learning Outcome (LO) and/or Knowledge and Understanding (K)/Aims | Links to the Play Cycle and Play Cycle Observation Method (PCOM) |
|---|---|---|
| **Play Environment** | Indoor and outdoor environments<br>Setting up for play<br>Accessible for play<br>Structured and unstructured play opportunities<br>Create play spaces with children<br>Support different types of play<br>Overcome barriers to children's play | Play Cycles occur in both indoor and outdoor spaces and for any type of play.<br>Providing children have access, or can create play spaces, Play Cycles will form and be observed.<br>The Play Cycle focuses on the process of play and can occur in both unstructured (child-led) and structured (adult-led) play. |
| **Resources and Activities** | Loose Parts<br>Resources<br>Activities<br>Planning<br>Support different types of play | The resources in the play environments (space) can stimulate the idea to play (pre-cure).<br>The more resources and loose parts, the more types of play can be engaged.<br>The resources relate to the Adult Intervention Style of simple involvement. The adult can facilitate play through providing resources. |
| **Child-Centred** | Child-centred approach<br>Risk<br>Verbal and non-verbal communication<br>Inclusion<br>Children's Rights<br>Freely-chosen play<br>Active participation | Child-centred play is supported where the child issues the play cue to initiate their freely chosen play.<br>The play cue can be verbal or non-verbal.<br>Children can play alone, or they can actively participate with other children and/or adults. |
| **Adult Intervention Style (AIS)** | Professional Practice<br>Effective communication<br>Relationship and trust<br>Intervention style<br>Respond to play cues<br>Be involved when appropriate<br>Facilitate play | The process of play is supported by one of four AIS of play maintenance, simple involvement, medial intervention, and complex intervention.<br>Adults may initiate play cues for both typically developed and atypically developed children<br>Both a passive involvement in the Play Cycle (play maintenance and simple involvement) and an active involvement (medial intervention and complex intervention) involves communication that can be verbal, as in responding to a play cue, or non-verbal through observing children play.<br>Be aware of how adult intervention can be controlling and adulterate the Play Cycle |

(Continued)

Table 6.4 Key areas, keywords, and the Play Cycle (Continued)

| Key Areas Around Play | Keywords with the Performance Criteria (P)/ Learning Outcome (LO) and/or Knowledge and Understanding (K)/Aims | Links to the Play Cycle and Play Cycle Observation Method (PCOM) |
|---|---|---|
| **Theory** | Supporting development<br>Supporting well-being<br>The six elements of the Play Cycle | The Play Cycle focuses on the process of play and relates to any type of play.<br>The six elements of the Play Cycle (pre-cue, play cue, play return, play frame, flow, and annihilation) provide theory that can support developmental theories.<br>Play can be naturally therapeutic supporting children's well-being and emotional development.<br>Play can support physical development through the play types of physical play and object play<br>Play can support cognitive development through the play types of symbolic play and games with rules<br>Play can support social development through the play type of pretend play |
| **Observations** | Observing children's play<br>Observing adult role<br>Recording and Planning | The Play Cycle Observation Method (PCOM) is one method of recording observations of how children play.<br>The PCOM can be used in conjunction with other methods.<br>The PCOM can be used for both typically and atypically developing children |
| **Reflective Practice** | Reflect on own and others practice<br>Reflect on how children play<br>Reflect on all elements of the Play Cycle<br>Evaluate on practice<br>Collect information on children's play<br>Research | When reflecting both in-action and on-action, the PCOM can provide information that can be used to reflect both own and other's practice.<br>The data from the PCOM can help evaluate and analyse practice<br>The data from the PCOM can be used to research how children play, types of play, the resources (loose parts) used, and the play space. |

on this course have three placements (one each year) and their placement is linked to Level 3 Children's Care Learning and Development through Social Care Wales. Another example is the Childhood Practice BA (Hons) (Scottish Level 10) where the degree offers practitioner status.

For students studying a higher education course that includes 'Practitioner Status', the NOS and the Play Cycle table can be used as both evidence and academic theory, with the key areas of Play Environment; Resources and Activities; Child-Centred; AIS; Theory; Observations; and Reflective Practice

> **Reflective Question**
>
> Read your relevant government play policy and strategy (for those in England, choose a play policy from one of the home nations). How does your practice using the Play Cycle and PCOM reflect play as defined in these government documents?
>
> If your setting has to adhere to the National Minimum Standards related to your country, how are you using the Play Cycle and PCOM to reflect the play-related standards?
>
> Can you map the Play Cycle and PCOM to your vocational qualification's Performance Criteria/Learning Outcomes and Knowledge, Skills, and Understanding/Aims? Remember to focus on the key aspects of Play Environment; Resources and Activities; Child-Centred; AIS; Theory; Observations; and Reflective Practice.

One student studying the BSc Early Childhood Studies with Practitioner Status at Swansea University reflected on the Play Cycle within their placement at a primary school with children aged 3 to 4 years of age:

> As the adult supporting the children's play, I learned it was important that I remained present. This is so that I could return a play cue, or I could provide resources to better support any Play Cycle that was ongoing. Secondly, I respected and understood the value of play for children so that I could provide a range of choices for them, act as a play partner, and anticipate what they needed in the process so that I could better support them in their play. In addition, it was crucial that I listened, trusted their choices, ensured their safety within the play, and consistently made opportunities for them within the environment with support from the practitioners in my setting. It was evident the abundant value play represented for the children, and I understood this better through learning about the play cycle as it enabled me a glimpse into the children's inner world thus, helping me understand their thought processes a s a little better.
>
> (Second Year BSc Early Childhood Studies Student)

## Conclusion

This chapter focused on how the Play Cycle and the PCOM can support play within government play policies and strategies, how it can support both practitioners and students who are studying for a vocational qualification and, in addition, how it can support practitioners in meeting the registration and inspection requirements in their settings.

Play within government play policies and strategies is based on Article 31, the Right to Play, within the UNCRC that promotes children's play to be freely chosen, and intrinsically motivated for no external reward or goal. The Play Cycle and the PCOM with the focus on the process of play reflect the position of play within these policies and strategies.

The PCOM provides evidence of the Play Cycle taking place. This could be used to support the registration and inspection of Ofsted (England), and Care Inspectorate Wales (CIW) (Wales) to provide evidence of supporting children's play as set out in each of the NMS.

# Conclusion
## A brief recap of the Play Cycle and potential challenges for professional practice

## Introduction

This book focuses on how the Play Cycle can support children's play and be part of reflective practice for practitioners and students in play-related contexts such as playwork, childcare, early years, and more inclusive settings, such as the children's ward in a hospital. The chapters in the book have covered the play environment, child-led play, Adult Intervention Styles (AIS), observing the Play Cycle using the Play Cycle Observation Method (PCOM), and how play is represented within legislation and policy. For the student and student practitioner, the different chapters are linked to vocational and higher education courses with a 'Practitioner Status' where the Play Cycle can be used to support the performance criteria and knowledge and understanding related to relevant National Occupational Standards (NOS).

## A brief recap

The Play Cycle focuses on the process of play (King & Newstead, 2021a) and consists of six elements: the pre-cue, play cue, play return, play frame, flow, and annihilation (King & Newstead, 2020; King & Sturrock, 2019). The book considers how the Play Cycle relates to:

- The hypothetical definition of play proposed by Neumann (1971)
- Play as a right under the United Nations Convention on the Rights of the Child (UNCRC) (UNICEF, 2007) reflected in government play policies and strategies (Office for First Minister and Deputy First Minister (OFMDFM), 2008; Scottish Government (SG), 2013; Welsh Government (WG), 2002, 2006)
- How the play environment is set up with as many loose parts (Nicholson, 1971) as possible to allow as many types of play to take place
- How the Play Cycle can promote child-led play (Shamsudin et al. 2021)
- How the adult can support child-led play from one of four types of intervention style: play maintenance; simple involvement, medial intervention, and complex intervention (Sturrock & Else, 1998; Sturrock et al., 2004)
- Both observational and reflective practice

The Play Cycle is a process that relates to child-led, collaborative, and adult-led play. The difference between these three aspects is how much control the child has over their play.

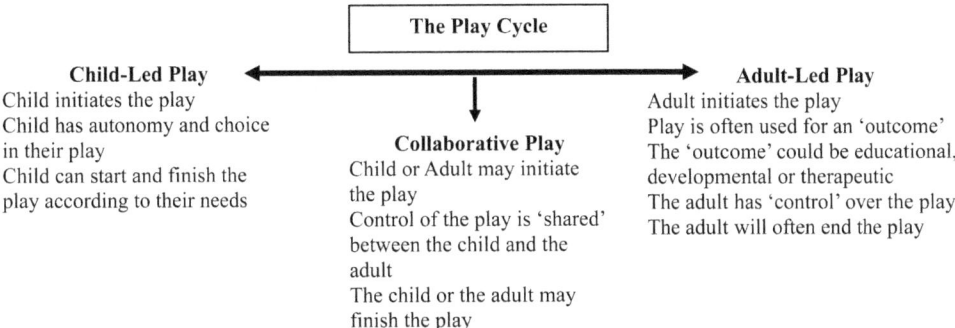

Figure C.1 Key aspects of child-led, adult-led, and collaborative play with the play cycle

Child-led play is often linked to free play (Bergen, 1988) where the adult leaves the content, choice, and type of play to the child, and only intervenes when requested, or for safeguarding reasons. The key aspects of child-led, collaborative, and adult-led play are summarised in Figure C.1.

Shamsudin (2021) explains play as 'not an activity for a serious purpose such as learning, but since it is a process-oriented activity, play supports children's learning indirectly' (p. 45). Adult-led play is often observed in early years education settings, for example, through the process of so-called play-based learning (Edwards & Cutter-Mackenzie, 2011; Pyle & Daniels, 2017) and is often associated with the concept of child-centred play (Cambell-Barr, 2019). However, whilst there is a perceived relationship between play and learning and development, often adult-led play focuses more on the 'learning' or 'development' rather than on the child, with the risk of play losing 'its nuances and benefits for children when the adults (e.g., educators, parents) are in control' (Shamsudin, 2021, p. 46).

King and Newstead (2021b), regarding Bronfenbrenner's (1992) Ecological Systems Theory, suggest that within the two systems closest to the playing child, the micro- and the meso-systems, the child has more control over the play when it is child-led, with the adult there to support, rather than lead, the process of play. When the play is adult-led, the adult can still focus on the process of play within the micro- and mesosystem, however, adult-led play usually has pre-determined outcomes to be met. These outcomes in adult-led play are often created in the two systems furthest from the child, the macro- and the exo-system, where play policies and legislation are constructed.

The play practitioner and student are often constrained by how play is being interpreted and used within policy, legislation, and professional qualifications, especially where play is focused on outcomes. There are potential challenges using the Play Cycle when considering how play is understood and applied, for example within an educational, recreational, and therapeutic context (Howard & McInnes, 2013).

> **Reflective Question**
>
> What do you think the challenges will be using the Play Cycle in your professional practice?

82  The Play Cycle in practice

The challenges of using a playwork approach within professional practice (which includes using the Play Cycle) include conflicting agendas on different perspectives of play, adult-led outcomes, and adult self-control (King & Newstead, 2024). These challenges are related to policy, legislation, professional qualifications, professional practice, and individual perceptions of play.

## The potential challenges in applying the Play Cycle in professional practice

The Play Cycle focuses on the process of play (King & Newstead, 2019). Play, as discussed within the book can also be focused on outcomes (educational or therapeutic), meeting registration standards, and vocational performance criteria. There could be a potential challenge in interpreting and/or implanting the Play Cycle when play is focused away from the process. The potential challenge of the Play Cycle in professional practice relates to how play is perceived within policy and legislation, how it is perceived in professional qualifications, the context in which play is being used, and individual perceptions of play. This is shown in Figure C.2.

## Play perceived in policy and legislation

The play policies and strategies published in Wales (Welsh Government (WG), 2002), Scotland (Scottish Government (SG), 2013), Northern Ireland (Office of the First Minister and Deputy First Minister (OFMDFM), 2008), and the Republic of Ireland (National Children's Office (NCO), 2004) focus on play being freely chosen and reflecting the child's right to play. This definition and application of play do not appear to be a challenge when applying the Play Cycle, where children's choice and control of their play is supported by adults. However, when the play policies refer to learning and development, the focus of play can then move from the 'process' to an 'outcome', and it is here that a potential challenge may exist.

The same challenge of freely chosen play and learning and development is also evident within the different National Minimum Standards (NMS). Whilst freely chosen play is stated in the NMS in Wales (WG, 2023) and Scotland (SG, 2017), play is linked to learning

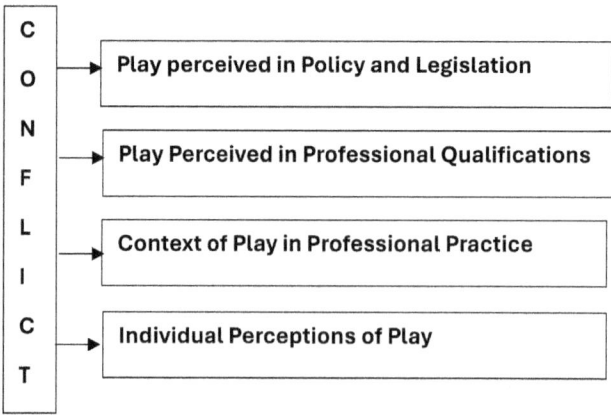

*Figure C.2* The Play Cycle and potential areas of challenge

and development which are more focused in the NMS of Northern Ireland (DoH, 2018) and the Republic of Ireland (TULSA, 2018). Another consideration concerning the NMS relates to the background and professional experience of the person undertaking the inspection. The inspector's professional background may, for example, be within education and their knowledge and understanding of play may therefore be based more on learning outcomes than on the power of play in its own right; this might influence their judgement of play-related NMS standards.

This challenge between the role of play between policy and practice within early years education in the United Kingdom (UK) has been identified and discussed by Wood (2013; 2022) and McInnes (2021). Play within educational curricula is 'central' (Black, 2023, p. 171) to learning, and 'policy and curricula outlines a view of play which is planned, purposeful and structured' (McInnes, 2021, p. 76) with a focus on outcomes. The focus on outcomes reflects an emphasis on more adult-led play, with adults having more control over children's play (King, 2025).

## Play perceived in professional qualifications

Vocational qualifications pose less of an issue with incorporating the Play Cycle in Playwork courses where the NOS are underpinned by the eight Playwork Principles (Playwork Principles Scrutiny Group (PPSG), 2005). For childcare-related vocational qualifications, there is again, more of a focus on children's learning and development, where aspects of the Play Cycle do appear in various vocational courses under the NOS, however, this mostly relates to supporting 'child-centred' play and considers play in terms of learning and development. In addition, the interpretation of the elements of the Play Cycle, most notably the play cue, play return, and play frame, do not match with the most up-to-date definitions of the six elements of the Play Cycle provided within this book. This point also relates to the current NOS in Playwork.

## Context of play in professional practice

Play will vary in the context in which it is being used as reflected in the seven rhetorics of play proposed by eminent play author, Sutton-Smith (1997). The seven rhetorics of play refer to speech or writing intended to be effective and to influence people, as follows:

- Play as progress where children develop through play
- Play as fate that is out of children's control
- Play as power, often applied to sports and contests
- Play as identity to confirm identity within a community
- Play as the imaginary that idealises the imagination and creativity
- Play of the self that may include solitary play and high-risk play
- Play as a frivolous activity considered as activities of the 'idle'

The Seven Rhetorics developed by Sutton-Smith aimed to 'bring some coherence to the ambiguous field of play theory' (p. 7), however, each rhetoric may have a different meaning and perception of play. Smith and Vollstedt (1985) stated that play researchers 'have come from a variety of backgrounds, covering the natural and biological sciences, the social sciences, and humanities' (p. 1042). This variety of backgrounds can be applied to professional practice where play has a different use and focus, for example, the practitioner who works within a recreational context may reflect the 'play as power' rhetoric, whereas practitioners employed in educational contexts may be more inclined to align with the rhetoric of 'play as progress' where play is used for a developmental outcome.

## Individual perceptions of play

For most adults, at some point in their childhood, they would have engaged in play. Play may have taken place at home, at school, in the streets, in the woods, on the beach, or maybe in a supervised provision such as an After School Club (ASC) or Adventure Playground (AP) (King, 2020b). How we play as children will help shape the individual perceptions of play we develop through adulthood as parents, teachers, playworkers, childcare workers, and early years practitioners. Differences in how play is perceived and understood exist between early years practitioners (McInnes et al., 2011), between teachers (Hyvönen, 2011), between parents (Warash et al., 2019), between parents and teachers (Rothlein & Brett, 1987), and between parents and child development professionals (Fisher et al., 2008). There are clear differences in how play is perceived by adults.

When adults have a strong view of play as being important for learning this may influence a more adult-led perception of play, and more emphasis on learning and development outcomes. Here, the process of play may not be deemed important. When adults are more aligned with a perception of child-led play being more important, more focus on the process of play, whether consciously or unconsciously, may dominate, and the adult may take on a more supportive role.

> **Reflective Question**
>
> How would you address any potential challenge in using the Play Cycle in your professional practice?

## Conclusion – A final thought

This chapter has considered areas of potential challenge of using the Play Cycle in four aspects: policy and legislation; vocational qualifications, professional practice, and individual perceptions of play. The knowledge, understanding, perception, and interpretation of play between these four areas will depend on expectations, outcomes, context, and requirements. What joins all these elements together is that play is a process, and using the Play Cycle can still be applied to policy, legislation, and professional practice, irrespective of where play is being used as a starting point, as a freely chosen process, or an educational outcome (assessment) (Howard & King, 2014).

A final thought. When we refer back to the 'Colorado Paper' (Sturrock & Else, 1998), which was where the Play Cycle was first proposed, the first paragraph and its definition of the term 'playworkers', whilst possibly only incidentally included, now takes on greater significance when considered the application of the Play Cycle far wider than playwork:

> Throughout this paper, we use the term playworker to describe adults active in playwork with children. Of course, this description is intended to include parents and other adults active in playing with children.
>
> (Sturrock & Else, 1998, p. 73)

The 'other adults' can be childcare workers, early years workers, teachers, teaching assistants, lunchtime supervisors, play therapists, hospital play staff, prison play staff, pre-school workers, nursery workers, childminders, and anybody else who works with children and young people in a play-based context. Whilst the Play Cycle was first introduced and developed within playwork, it is intended to be inclusive; after all, playwork does not 'own the rights' of the Play Cycle. The aim of this book is to make the Play Cycle accessible for any practitioner or student who is working or studying in a play-related context to support and reflect on children's play.

The final words are left to this playworker who sums up the positive impact introducing the Play Cycle has had on their professional practice:

> The Play Cycle is a complex concept which helps to describe the daily workings of play environments and the deep meaning in the everyday acts of children's play. The sharing of this concept has meant that playworkers have a common language in which we can start conversations and evaluate our work. The depth and meaning of the beautiful and lyrical flow of the Colorado Paper acts as an invitation for playworkers to value the work we do and to respect the meaning and purpose of children's rich inner worlds. Sturrock and Else have pulled off the conjuring trick of telling us what we already knew but didn't have the words to describe. The paper has been particularly useful for me in considering the cues that certain children make that are badly made and that nearly always produce unhappiness and violence. When inexperienced playworkers talk of children as "bad" and their acts as "mean", I am able to talk about play cues and how some children, who are suffering, are giving off cues that repel others. In this knowledge we are able to attempt to support an environment which can help children who are suffering, we can return to them with a response that may be healing.
>
> Playworker

# APPENDIX

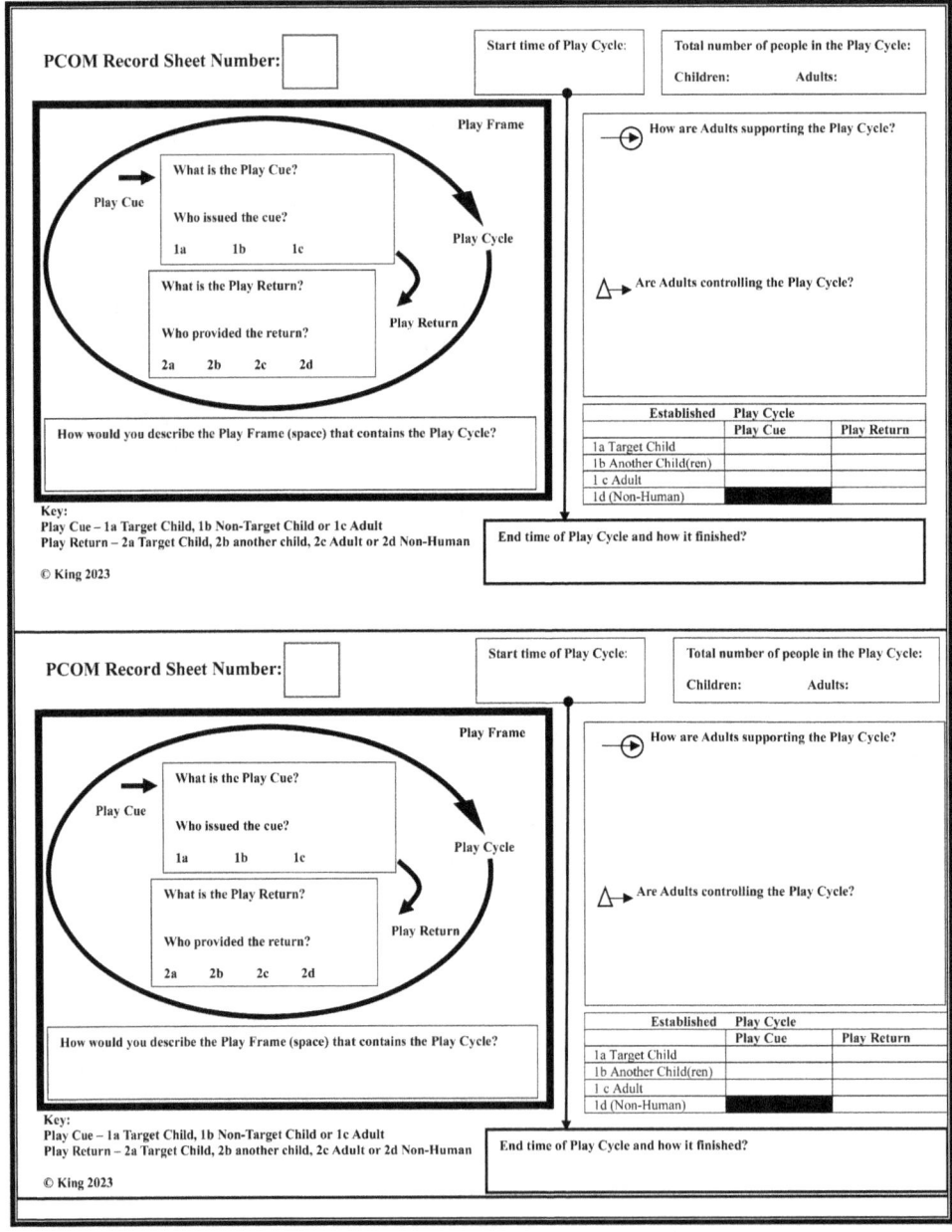

Figure A.1 Play Cycle Observation Method (PCOM) Record Sheet

Appendix 87

Table A.1 Play Cycle Observation Method (PCOM) Record Sheet Table

| Record Sheet | Play Cue Issued ||||Play Return ||||Time | Play Cues in Established Play Cycles ||||
|---|---|---|---|---|---|---|---|---|---|---|---|---|
| | Column 1 | Column 2 | Column 3 | | Column 4 ||| Column 5 | Column 6 | Column 7 | | Column 8 |
| | TC | N-TC | A | TC | N-TC | A | N-H | | TC | N-TC | | A |
| PCOM 1 | | | | | | | | | | | | |
| PCOM 2 | | | | | | | | | | | | |
| PCOM 3 | | | | | | | | | | | | |
| PCOM 4 | | | | | | | | | | | | |
| PCOM 5 | | | | | | | | | | | | |
| PCOM 6 | | | | | | | | | | | | |
| PCOM 7 | | | | | | | | | | | | |
| PCOM 8 | | | | | | | | | | | | |
| PCOM 9 | | | | | | | | | | | | |
| PCOM 10 | | | | | | | | | | | | |
| PCOM 11 | | | | | | | | | | | | |
| PCOM 12 | | | | | | | | | | | | |
| PCOM 13 | | | | | | | | | | | | |
| PCOM 14 | | | | | | | | | | | | |
| PCOM 15 | | | | | | | | | | | | |
| PCOM 16 | | | | | | | | | | | | |
| PCOM 17 | | | | | | | | | | | | |
| PCOM 18 | | | | | | | | | | | | |
| PCOM 19 | | | | | | | | | | | | |
| PCOM 20 | | | | | | | | | | | | |
| Add Up Each Column | TC Play Cues | N-TC Play Cues | A Play Cues | Play Cycles Formed (Add All the Returns Together) |||| Add All Times Together | TC Play Cues | N-TC Play Cues | | A Play Cues |
| Total | | | | | | | | | | | | |
| Average | | | | | | | | | | | | |

Key: TC = Target Child; N-TC = Non-Target Child; A = Adult; N-H = Non-Human (e.g., object)

*Table A.2* Play Cycle Observation Method (PCOM) Frequency and Percentage Table

| PCOM Record Sheet Number: | | Frequency | Percentage |
|---|---|---|---|
| **Play Cues Issued By** | Target Child | | |
| | Non-Target Child | | |
| | Adult | | |
| **Play Returns Given** | Target Child | | |
| | Non-Target Child | | |
| | Adult | | |
| | Non-Human | | |
| **Play Cycle Formed** | | | |
| **Average Length of Play Cycles** | | | |
| **Play Cues in Established Play Cycle** | Target Child | | |
| | Non-Target Child | | |
| | Adult | | |

# REFERENCES

Acer, D., Gözen, G., First, Z. S., Kefeli, H., & Aslan, B. (2016). Effects of a Redesigned Classroom on Play Behaviour Among Preschool Children. Early Child Development and Care, 186(12), 1907-1925.
Ahuja, S., & Saha, A. (2016). They Lead, You Follow: Role of Non-Directive Play Therapy in Building Resilience. Journal of Psychosocial Research, 11(1), 167-175.
Aksoy, A. B., & Aksoy, M. K. (2017). The Role of Block Play in Early Childhood. In Koleva, I., & Duman, G. (Eds.) Educational Research and Practice (pp. 104-113). Sofia: St. Kliment Ohridski University Press.
Aksoy, M., & Aksoy, A. B. (2022). An Investigation on the Effects of Block Play on the Creativity of Children, Early Child Development and Care, DOI: 10.1080/03004430.2022.2071266
Amani, J., & Fussy, D. S. (2023). Balancing Child-Centered and Teacher-Centred Didactic Approaches in Early Years Learning, Education, 3-13, https://www.tandfonline.com/doi/epub/10.1080/14681366.2021.1955736
Andreasson, F., Gentile, A. D., Backman, & Klintwall, L. (2023). Child-Directed Play With Mothers of Young Autistic Children: A Study on the Benefits of the Approach. GAP, 24(1). 54-65.
Axline, V. M. (1947). Play Therapy. New York: Ballantine Books.
Axline, V. M. (1964). Dibs: In Search of Self. London: Penguin Books.
Baines, E., & Blatchford, P. (2019). School Break and Lunch Times and Young People's Social Lives: A Follow-Up National Study. Retrieved from https://discovery.ucl.ac.uk/id/eprint/10073916/1/Baines%2042402%20BreaktimeSurvey%20-%20Main%20public%20report%20%28May19%29-Final.pdf.
Ball, D., Gill, T., & Spiegal, B. (2013) Managing Risk in Play Provision: Implementation Guide (2nd edition). http://www.playengland.org.uk/media/172644/managing-risk-in-play-provision.pdf.
Barrouillet, P. (2015). Theories of Cognitive Development: From Piaget to Today. Developmental Review, 38, 1-12.
Benjamin, J. (1961). In Search of Adventure: A Study of the Junk Playground. London: NCSS.
Bergen, D. (1988). Using a Schema for Play and Learning. In D. Bergen (Ed.) Play as a Medium for Learning and Development. A Handbook of Theory and Practice (pp. 169-180). Portsmouth New Hampshire: Heinemann Educational Books.
Black, E. (2023). Childhood Practice: A Reflective & Evidence-Based Approach. In M. Carroll & M. Wingrave (Eds.) Playful Pedagogy (pp. 165-178). London: SAGE.
Bronfenbrenner, U. (1992). Ecological Models of Human Development. In M. Gauvain & M. Colde (Eds.) International Encyclopedia of Education, Volume 3, 2nd Edition (pp. 37-43). Freeman.
Brussoni, M., Olsen, L. L., Pike, I., & Sleet, D. A. (2012). Risky Play and Children's Safety: Balancing Priorities for Optimal Child Development. International Journal of Environmental Research and Public Health, 9, 3134-3148.
Çakırer, H. B., & Garcia, I. G. (2010). A Qualitative Study on Play Corners: Comparison of a Semi-Private Preschool and a Public Preschool in Catalonia, Spain. Procedia Social and Behavioural Sciences, 5, 590-594.
Campbell-Barr, V. (2019). Interpretations of Child Centred Practice in Early Childhood Education and Care. COMPARE, 49(2), 249-265.
Campbell-Barr, V. (2021). The Provision, Protection and Participation of Children's Rights in Professional Practice. In A. Višnjić-Jevtić, A. R. Sadownik & I. Engdahl (Eds.) Young Children in the World and Their Rights: Thirty Years With the United Nations Convention on the Rights of the Child (pp. 221-233). New York: Springer.

Cankaya, O., Rohatyn-Martin, N., Leach, J., Taylor, K., & Bulut, O. (2023). Preschool Children's Loose Parts Play and the Relationship to Cognitive Development: A Review of the Literature. Journal of Intelligence, 11(151), 1-19.

Canning, N. (2007). Children's Empowerment in Play. European Early Childhood Education Research Journal, 15(2), 227-236.

Canning, N. (2020). The Significance of children's Play and Empowerment: An Observational Tool: In TACTYC Occassional Paper Series Occassional Paper 14. TACTYC.

Care Inspectorate (2021). A Quality Framework for Daycare of Children, Childminding and School Aged Childcare. Retrieved from https://www.careinspectorate.com/images/documents/6585/Quality%20framework%20for%20early%20learning%20and%20childcare%202022_PRINT%20FRIENDLY.pdf.

Carroll, G., & Boutall, T. (2011). Guide to Developing National Occupational Standards. Retrieved from https://assets.publishing.service.gov.uk/media/5a7dd27ce5274a5eb14e7657/nos-guide-for-_developers-2011.pdf.

Casey, T., & Robertson, J. (2016). Loose Parts: A Toolkit. Edinburgh: Inspiring Scotland.

Casper, R., Shloim, N., & Hebron, J. (2021). Use of non-Directive Therapy for Adolescents With Autism spectrum Disorder: A Systematic Review. Counselling Psychotherapy Research, 23, 300–312.

Çelebi̇, A., Aytekİn, A., Küçükoğlu, S., & Çelebİoğlu, A. (2015). Hospitalized Children and Play. İzmir Dr. Behçet Uz Çocuk Hast. Dergisi, 5(3):156-160.

Cheung, R. H. P. (2017) Teacher-Directed Versus Child-Centred: the Challenge of Promoting Creativity in Chinese Preschool Classrooms, Pedagogy, Culture & Society, 25(1), 73-86, DOI: 10.1080/14681366.2016.1217253.

City & Guilds (2018). SVQ 3 Social Services (Children and Young People) at SCQF level 7 (4174-03). Retrieved from https://secure.sqa.org.uk/sqa/files_ccc/Information_Sheet_SSCYP_level3.pdf

City & Guilds (2019a). City & Guilds Level 2 Diploma for the Early Years Practitioner (England) (4228-02). Retrieved from https://www.cityandguilds.com/-/media/productdocuments/children/children_and_young_people/4228/centre_documents/4228-02_l2_diploma_early_years_practitioner_qualification_handbook_v2-pdf.ashx.

City & Guilds (2019b). City & Guilds Level 2 Diploma in Children's Care Learning and Development (Northern Ireland) (3087-02). Retrieved from https://www.cityandguilds.com/-/media/product-documents/children/children_and_young_people/3087/centre-documents/3087_l2-diploma-in-ccld-northern-ireland-handbook.ashx.

City & Guilds (2020). Retrieved from https://www.cityandguilds.com/-/media/productdocuments/children/children_and_young_people/3087/centre-documents/l3-diploma-in-ccld-northern-irelandqhbv1-pdf.ashx.

City & Guilds (2021). Level 3 Diploma for the Early Years Practitioner (Early Years Educator) 3605-03. Retrieved from https://www.cityandguilds.com/qualifications-and-apprenticeships/children/children-and-young-people/3605-early-years-practitioner-early-years-educator-and-early-years-and-childcare#tab=information

City & Guilds/WFEC (2024). City & Guilds Level 5 Leadership and Management of Children's Care, Play, Learning and Development: Practice. Retrieved from https://www.healthandcarelearning.wales/media/owuoc1te/18_l5_ccpld_practice_qualification_specification_english_v12-apr24.pdf.

City & Guilds/WJEC (2020a). Level 3 Children's Care, Play, Learning and Development: Practice and Theory Learner Information Guide. Retrieved from https://www.healthandcarelearning.wales/media/gv0dqrtl/level-3-ccpld-learner-guide.pdf.

City & Guilds/WJEC (2020b). WJEC Level 2 Children's Care, Play, Learning & Development: Core. Retrieved from https://www.healthandcarelearning.wales/media/wisl5kcf/wjec-ccpld-core-specification-first-assessment-2024-e.pdf.

City & Guilds/WJEC (2020c). WJEC Level 2 Children's Care, Play, Learning & Development: Practice. Retrieved from https://www.healthandcarelearning.wales/media/iawhicbo/l2-ccpld-practice-handbook-english_v12.pdf.

City & Guilds/WJEC (2020d). WJEC Level 2 Children's Care, Play, Learning & Development: Practice & Theory. Retrieved from https://www.wjec.co.uk/media/p01dgm24/cppld-practice-and-theory-spec.pdf.

City & Guilds/WJEC (2020e). WJEC Level 3 Children's Care, Play, Learning & Development: Practice. Retrieved from https://www.healthandcarelearning.wales/media/gikftp2h/l3-ccpld-practice-handbook-english_29-oct.pdf

City & Guilds/WJEC (2020f). WJEC Level 3 Children's Care, Play, Learning & Development: Practice and Theory. Retrieved from https://www.healthandcarelearning.wales/media/llkots0e/l3-ccpld-practice-and-theory-specification-e-200923.pdf

City & Guilds/WJEC (2021a). Level 4 Preparing for Leadership and Management in Children's Care, Play, Learning and Development. Retrieved from https://www.healthandcarelearning.wales/qualifications/level-4-preparing-for-leadership-and-management-in-childrens-care-play-learning-and-development/

City & Guilds/WJEC (2021b). Level 4 Professional Practice in Children's Care, Play, Learning and Development. Retrieved from https://ccea.org.uk/downloads/docs/ccea-asset/Curriculum/Learning%20through%20Play%20in%20Pre-School%20and%20Foundation%20Stage_0.pdf

Cogher, L. (1999). The Use of non-Directive Play in Speech and Language Therapy. Child Language Teaching and Therapy, 15(1), 7-15.

Common Threads (2024). PARS courses for all. Retrieved from https://www.parsplaywork.com/courses.

Conn, C. (2013). Autism and the Social World of Childhood. London: Routledge.

Conn, C. (2014). Autism and the Social World of Childhood. London: Routledge.

Costall, A. (1995). Socializing Affordance. Theory & Psychology, 5 (4), 467-481. doi: 10.1177/0959354395054001

Council for the Curriculum, Examinations and Assessment (2022). Learning through Play in Pre-School and Foundation Stage. Retrieved from https://ccea.org.uk/downloads/docs/ccea-asset/Curriculum/Learning%20through%20Play%20in%20Pre-School%20and%20Foundation%20Stage_0.pdf.

Cranwell, K. (2003). Towards a History of Adventure Playgrounds 1931-2000. In N. Norman (Ed.) (2003). An Architecture of Play: A Survey of London's Adventure Playgrounds (pp. 17-26). Retrieved from http://www.play-scapes.com/wp-content/uploads/2015/03/Architecture-Of-Play1.pdf.

Csikszentmihalyi, M. (1975). Beyond Boredom and Anxiety: The Experience of Play in Work and Games.

Dekkers, T. J., de Water, E., & Scheres, A. (2022). Impulsive and Risky Decision-Making in Adolescents With Attention-deficit/hyperactivity Disorder (ADHD): The Need for a Developmental Perspective. Current Opinion in Psychology, 44, 330-336.

Department for Education (2023). Early years foundation stage statutory framework For group and school-based providers Setting the standards for learning, development and care for children from birth to five. Retrieved from https://assets.publishing.service.gov.uk/media/65aa5e42ed27ca001327b2c7/EYFS_statutory_framework_for_group_and_school_based_providers.pdf.

Department of Health and Social Services (DoH) and the Office of Law Reform (2018). CHILDREN (NI) ORDER 1995: Guidance and Regulations Volume 2 Family Support, Child Minding And Day Care. Retrieved from https://www.health-ni.gov.uk/sites/default/files/publications/health/children-ni.order-95-guidance.PDF.

Dewey, J., & Bentley, A. F. (1949). Knowing and the Known. Boston: Beacon Press.

Dodd, H. F., & Lester, K. J. (2021). Adventurous Play as a Mechanism for Reducing Risk for Childhood Anxiety: A Conceptual Model. Clinical Child and Family Psychology Review, 24(1), 164-181.

Dodd, H. F., Nesbit, R. J., & FitzGibbon, L. (2022). Child's Play: Examining the Association Between Time Spent Playing and Child Mental Health. Child Psychiatry & Human Development, 54, 1678-1686.

Edwards, G., & Thomas, G. (2010) Can Reflective Practice Be Taught?, Educational Studies, 36:4, 403-414, DOI: 10.1080/03055690903424790.

Edwards, S., & Cutter-Mackenzie, A. (2011). Environmentalising Early Childhood Education Curriculum Through Pedagogies of Play. Australasian Journal of Early Childhood, 36(1), 51-59.

Eisele, & Howard (2012) Exploring the Presence of Characteristics Associated With Play Within the Ritual Repetitive Behaviour of Autistic Children. International Journal of Play, 1(2), 139-150.

Fahy, S., Delicâte, N., & Lynch, H. (2021) Now, Being, Occupational: Outdoor Play and Children With Autism, Journal of Occupational Science, 28(1), 114-132, DOI: 10.1080/14427591.2020.1816207.

Feiten, T. E. (2020). Mind after Uexküll: A Foray Into the Worlds of Ecological Psychologists and Enactivists. Frontiers in Psychology, 11, Article 480. https://doi.org/10.3389/fpsyg.2020.00480

Fisher, K. R., Hirsh-Pasek, K., Golinkoff, R. M., & Gryfe, S. G. (2008). Conceptual split? Parents' and experts' Perceptions of Play in the 21st Century. Journal of Applied Developmental Psychology. 29(4), 305-316.

Flannigan, C., & Dietze, B. (2017). Children, Outdoor Play, and Loose Parts. Journal of Childhood Studies, 42(4), 53-60.

Garden, A., & Downes, G. (2023). A Systematic Review of Forest Schools Literature in England, Education 3-13, 51:2, 320-336, DOI:10.1080/03004279.2021.1971275.

Garvey, C. (1990). Play (enlarged edition). Cambridge, Massachusetts: Harvard University Press.

Gibbs, G. (1988). Learning By Doing. London: Further Education Unit.

Gibson, J. J. (1986). The Ecological Approach to Visual Perception. Hillsdale, NJ: Lawrence Erlbaum Associates.

Gibson, J. L., Cornell, M., & Gill, T. (2017). A Systematic Review of Research into the Impact of Loose Parts Play on Children's Cognitive, Social and Emotional Development. School Mental Health, 9, 295-309.

Gov.ie (2016). Child Care Act 1991 (Early Years Services) Regulations 2016. Retrieved from https://assets.gov.ie/34528/d51d93d029bc44f7883d41b25d98e890.pdf.

Government of Ireland (2019). First 5: A Whole-of-Government Strategy for Babies, Young Children and Their Families 2019-2028. Dublin: Government of Ireland.

Groos, K. (1901). The Play of Man. London: William Heinemann.

Gull, C., Bogunovich, J., Goldstein, S. L., & Rosengarten, T. (2019). Definitions of Loose Parts in Early Childhood Outdoor Classrooms: A Scoping Review. The International Journal of Early Childhood Environmental Education, 6(3), 37-52.

Hall, G. S. (1905). Adolescence: Its Psychology and Its Relations to Physiology, Anthropology, Sociology, Sex, Crime, Religion and Education. New York: D. Appleton and Company.

Hateli, B. (2021). The Effect of non-Directive Play Therapy on Reduction of Anxiety Disorders in Young Children. Counselling Psychotherapy Research, 22, 140-146.

Health and Safety Executive (HSE) (2012) Children's Play and Leisure – Promoting A Balanced Approach. https://www.hse.gov.uk/entertainment/assets/docs/childrens-play-july-2012.pdf

Hébert, C., (2015). Knowing and/or Experiencing: a Critical Examination of the Reflective Models of John Dewey and Donald Schön. Reflective Practice, 16(3), 361-371.

Heft, H. (2003) Affordances, Dynamic Experience, and the Challenge of Reification. Ecological Psychology, 15(2), 149-180.

Holloway, S. L., & Pimlott-Wilson, H. (2017). Reconceptualising Play: Balancing Childcare, Extra-Curricular Activities and Free Play in Contemporary Childhoods. Transactions of the Institute of British Geographers, 43, 420-434.

Homeyer, L. E., & Morrison, M. O. (2008). Play Therapy: Practice, Issues, and Trends. American Journal of Play, 1, 210-228.

Houser, N. E., Cawley, J., Kolen, A. M., Rainham, D., Rehman, L., Turner, J., Kirk, S. F. L., & Stone, M. R. (2019). A Loose Parts Randomized Controlled Trial to Promote Active Outdoor Play in Preschool-Aged Children: Physical Literacy in the Early Years (PLEY) Project. Methods and Protocols, 2(27), 1-14.

Houser, N. E., Roach, L. O., Stone, M. R., Turner, J., & Kirk, S. F. L. (2016). Let the Children Play: Scoping Review on the Implementation and Use of Loose Parts for Promoting Physical Activity Participation. Public Health, 3(4), 781-799.

Howard, J. (2002). Eliciting Children's Perceptions of Play, Work and Learning Using the Activity Apperception Story Procedure. Early Child Development and Care, 172, 489-502.

Howard, J., & King, P. (2014). Re-Establishing Early Years Practitioners as Play Professions. In J. Moyles (Ed.) The Excellence of Play (pp. 125-137). Maidenhead: Open University Press.

Howard, J., & McInnes, K. (2013) The Essence of Play. London: Routledge.

Hughes, B. (2002) A Playworker's Taxonomy of Play Types, 2nd edition, London: PlayLink.

Hughes, B. (2002). Evolutionary Playwork and Reflective Analytical Practice. London: Routledge.

Hughes, B. (2012). Evolutionary Playwork Second Edition. London: Routledge.

Hughes, L., & Cooper, P. (2007). Understanding and Supporting Children With ADHD: Strategies for Teachers, Parents and Other Professionals. London: Paul Chapman Publishing.

Hyvönen, P., & Juujärvi, M. (2005). Affordances of Playful Environment: A View of Finnish Girls and Boys. In P. Kommers & G. Richards (Eds.) Proceedings of World Conference on Educational Multimedia, Hypermedia and Telecommunications (pp. 1563-1572). Chesapeake, VA: AACE.

Hyvönen, P. T. (2011). Play in the School Context? The Perspectives of Finnish Teachers. Australian Journal of Teacher Education, 36(8). 49-67, https://doi.org/10.14221/ajte.2011v36n8.5.

IK Commission for Employment and Skills (2011). NOS Strategy 2010-2020. Retrieved from https://assets.publishing.service.gov.uk/media/5a7cf94340f0b60aaa2936d5/nos-strategy-2011.pdf.

Irish Statute Book (2013). Child and Family Agency Act 2013. Retrieved from https://www.irishstatutebook.ie/eli/2013/act/40/enacted/en/pdf.

Jarrold, C. (2004). A Review of Research into Pretend Play in Autism. Autism, 7, 379-390.

Josefi, O., & Ryan, V. (2004). Non-Directive Play Therapy for Young Children With Autism: A Case Study. Clinical Child Psychology and Psychiatry, 9(4), 533-551.

Jun-Tai, N. (2008). Play in hospital. Paediatrics and Child Health, 18(5), 233–237.

Kalyva, E. (2011). Autism: Educational & Therapeutic Approaches. London: SAGE.

King, P. (2020a). Adult Memories of Attending After-School Club Provision as a Child Between 1990 and 2010, Child Care in Practice,

King, P. (2020b). The Play Cycle Observation Method (PCOM): A Pilot Study. International Journal of Playwork Practice, 1(1), Article 1. https://doi.org/10.25035/ijpp.01.01.02. DOI:10.1080/13575279.2020.1792839.

King, P. (2021a). How Have Adventure Playgrounds in the United Kingdom Adapted Post-March Lockdown in 2020? International Journal of Playwork Practice, 2(1), Article 5-1-37.

King, P. (2021b). How Have after-School Clubs Adapted in the United Kingdom Post-March Lockdown? Journal of Childhood, Education & Society, 2(2), 106–116.

King, P. (2022a). How Has Covid-19 Impacted on Playwork – One Year on from Returning from Lockdown, Child Care in Practice, DOI: 10.1080/13575279.2022.2084365.

King, P. (2022b). A Theoretical Expansion off the Play Cycle: Jakob Von Uexküll's Functional Cycle and the Perceptual Cue. American Journal of Play, 14(1), 173-187.

King, P. (2023). Flow and the Play Cycle: A Theoretical Consideration of the Importance of Flow in Established Play Cycles. American Journal of Play, 15(2), 179-195.

King, P. (2025). Play-Based Learning and the Play Cycle: A Consideration of the Adult Role in the Process of Play Within Play-Based Learning. American Journal of Play, 17(3).

King, P., Atkins, L., & Burr, B. (2021). Piloting the Play Cycle Observation Method in 'real time': Recording children's Play Cycles in pre-School Provision. Journal of Early Childhood Research, 19(3), 298-308. https://doi.org/10.1177/1476718X20969851.

King, P., & Howard, J. (2014). Factors Influencing children's Perceptions of Choice Within Their Free Play Activity: the Impact of Functional, Structural and Social Affordances. Journal of Playwork Practice, 1(2), 173–90.

King, P., Howard, J., Ashton, K., & Fung, S. (2016). Junk Modeling at the British Science Festival: A Reflection on non-Directive Play in Action. Journal of Playwork Practice, 3(2), 149-54.

King, P., & Sills-Jones (2018). Children's Use of Public Spaces and the Role of the Adult – A Comparison of Play Ranging in the UK, and the leikkipuisto (Play Parks) in Finland, International Journal of Play, 7(1), 27-40.

King, P., & Newstead, S. (2020). Re-Defining the Play Cycle: An Empirical Study of Playworkers' Understanding of Playwork Theory. Journal of Early Childhood Research, 18(1), 99-111

King, P., & Newstead, S. (2021a). Understanding the Adult Role in the Play Cycle—an Empirical Study. Child Care in Practice, 27(3), 212-223

King, P., & Newstead, S. (2021c). Conclusion. In P. King & S. Newstead (Eds.) Play Across Childhood: International Perspectives on Diverse Contexts of Play (pp. 209–220). London: Springer. – need to change reference to c in chapter when found 27/8/24

King, P., & Newstead, S. (2022a). Childcare Worker's Understanding of the Play Cycle Theory: Can a Focus on "Process Not Product" Contribute to Quality Childcare Experiences? Child Care in Practice, 28(2), 164-177.

King, P., & Newstead, S. (2022b). A Comparison of Playworkers and Non-Playworkers Who Use a Playwork Approach, Child Care in Practice, DOI:10.1080/13575279.2022.2098255.

King, P., & Newstead, S. (2024). The Benefits and Challenges in Using a Playwork Approach. Child Care in Practice,

King, P., & Sturrock, G. (2019). The Play Cycle: Theory, Research and Application. London: Routledge.

King, P., & Temple, S. (2018) Transactional Analysis and the Ludic Third (TALT): A Model of Functionally Fluent Reflective Play Practice, Transactional Analysis Journal, 48(3), 258-271, DOI: 10.1080/03621537.2018.1471292.

King, P., & Newstead, S. (2021b) Demographic Data and Barriers to Professionalisation in Playwork, Journal of Vocational Education & Training, 73(4), 591-604, DOI:10.1080/13636820.2020.1744694.

Kleppe, R., Melhuish, E., & Sandseter, E. B. H. (2017). Identifying and Characterizing Risky Play in the Age One-to-Three Years, European Early Childhood Education Research Journal, 25(3), 370-385, DOI: 10.1080/1350293X.2017.1308163.

Kossyvaki, L., & Papoudi, D. (2016). A Review of Play Interventions for Children with Autism at School, International Journal of Disability, Development and Education, 63(1), https://doi.org/10.1080/1034912X.2015.1111303

Koukourikos, K., Tzeha, L., Pantelidou, P., & Tsaloglidou, A. (2015). The Importance of Play During Hospitalization of Children. Mater Sociomed, 27(6), 438-441.

Krasnor, L. R., & Pepler, D. J. (1980). The Study of children's Play: Some Suggested Future Directions. In K. H. Rubin (Ed.) New Directions for Child Development: Children's Play (pp. 85-95). San Francisco: Jossey-Bass.

Krason, K., & Szafraniec, G. (1999). Directive and Non-Directive Movement in Child Therapy. Early Child Development and Care, 158, 31-42.

Kyratzis, A. (2007) Using the Social Organizational Affordances of Pretend Play in American Preschool Girls' Interactions, Research on Language and Social Interaction, 40:4, 321-352, DOI: 10.1080/08351810701471310

Kyttä, M. (2002). Affordances of children's Environments in the Context of Cities, Small Towns, Suburbs and Rural Villages in Finland and Belarus. Journal of Environmental Psychology, 22, 109-123.

Kyttä, M. (2004). The Extent of Children's Independent Mobility and the Number of Actualized Affordances as Criteria for Child-Friendly Environments. Journal of Environmental Psychology, 24, 175-198.

Laaksoharju, T., Rape, E., & Kaivola, T. (2012). Garden Affordances for Social Learning, Play, and for Building Nature-Child Relationship. Urban Forestry & Urban Greening, 11, 195-203.

Lady Allen of Hurtwood (1967). Planning for Play. Massachusetts: MIP Press.

Lefebvre, H. (1991). The production of space (D. Nicholson-Smith, Trans.). London: Blackwell.

Legilsation.gov. (1989). Children Act 1989. Retrieved from https://www.legislation.gov.uk/ukpga/1989/41/pdfs/ukpga_19890041_en.pdf.

Legilsation.gov (2006). Childcare Act 2006. Retrieved from https://www.legislation.gov.uk/ukpga/2006/21/pdfs/ukpga_20060021_en.pdf.

Legilsation.gov. (2010a). Children and Families (Wales) Measure 2010. Retrieved from https://www.legislation.gov.uk/mwa/2010/1/pdfs/mwa_20100001_en.pdf.

Legislation.gov (1978). National Health Service (Scotland) Act 1978. Retrieved from National Health Service (Scotland) Act 1978. Retrieved from https://www.legislation.gov.uk/ukpga/1978/29/pdfs/ukpga_19780029_en.pdf.

Legislation.gov. (2000). Care Standards Act 2000. Retrieved from https://www.legislation.gov.uk/ukpga/2000/14/pdfs/ukpga_20000014_en.pdf.

Legislation.gov (2004). Children Act 2004. Retrieved from https://www.legislation.gov.uk/ukpga/2004/31/pdfs/ukpga_20040031_en.pdf.

Legislation.gov (2010b). Public Services Reform (Scotland) Act 2010. Retrieved from https://www.legislation.gov.uk/asp/2010/8/pdfs/asp_20100008_en.pdf.

Legislation.gov (2016). Regulation of Child Minding and Day Care (Wales) Order 2016. Retrieved from https://www.legislation.gov.uk/wsi/2016/98/pdfs/wsi_20160098_mi.pdf.

Legislation.gov.uk (1995a). Children (Scotland) Act 1995. Retrieved from https://www.legislation.gov.uk/ukpga/1995/36/data.pdf.

Legislation.gov.uk (1995b). Children (Northern Ireland) Order 1995. Retrieved from https://www.legislation.gov.uk/nisi/1995/755.

Legislation.gov.uk (2021a). Children (Scotland) Act 1995. Retrieved from https://www.legislation.gov.uk/ukpga/1995/36/data.pdf.

Lifter, K., Mason, E. J., Cannarella, A. M., & Cameron, A. D. (2022). Developmental Play Assessment for Practitioners (DPA-P) Guidebook and Training Website. New York: Routledge.

Lindon, J. (2010). Child-Initiated Learning: Positive Relationships in the Early Years. Retrieved from http://fplreflib.findlay.co.uk/books/1/FilesSamples/267497819092802_00000000698.pdf.

Lindon, J., & Trodd, J. (2016). Reflective Practice and Early Years Professionalism, 3rd Edition: Linking Theory and Practice. London: Hodder Education.

Marsh, J., Plowman, L., Yamada-Rice, D., Bishop, J., & Scott, F. (2016). Digital Play: a New Classification, Early Years, 36:3, 242-253, DOI: 10.1080/09575146.2016.1167675.

Mastrangelo, S. (2009). Play and the Child with Autism Spectrum Disorder: From Possibilities to Practice. International Journal of Play Therapy, 18(1), 13-30.

Maynard, T. (2007). Forest Schools in Great Britain: an Initial Exploration. Contemporary Issues in Early Childhood 8(4), 320-331.

Maynard, T., Waters, J., & Clement, J. (2013). Child-Initiated Learning, the Outdoor Environment and the 'underachieving' Child, Early Years, 33(3), 212-225. DOI:10.1080/09575146.2013.771152

McInnes, K. (2021). In P. King & S. Newstead (Eds.) Play Across Childhood: International Perspectives on Diverse Contexts of Play (73-96). London: Palgrave Macmillan.

McInnes, K., Howard, J., Crowley, K., & Miles, G. (2013). The Nature of Adult–Child Interaction in the Early Years Classroom: Implications for children's Perceptions of Play and Subsequent Learning Behaviour, European Early Childhood Education Research Journal, 21(2), 268–282, DOI: 10.1080/1350293X.2013.789194.

McInnes, K., Howard, J., Miles, G., & Crowley, K. (2011). Differences in practitioners' Understanding of Play and How This Influences Pedagogy and children's Perceptions of Play, Early Years, 31:2, 121–133, DOI: 10.1080/09575146.2011.572870.

McKendrick, J. H., Loebach, J., & Casey, T. (2018). Realizing Article 31 Through General Comment No. 17: Overcoming Challenges and the Quest for an Optimum Play Environment. Children, Youth and Environments, 28(2), 1–11.

Mohajan, H. K. (2017). Roles of Communities of Practice for the Development of the Society. Journal of Economic Development, Environment and People, 6(3), 1–23.

National Council for Curriculum and Assessment (2009). Aistear: The Early Childhood Curriculum Framework Guidelines for Good Practice: Retrieved from https://ncca.ie/media/6306/guidelines-for-good-practice.pdf.

National Playing Fields Association (2000). Children's Play Council & PlayLink: In Best Play: What Play Provision Should Do for Children. London: NPFA.

NCFE CACHE (2022). Qualification Specification: NCFE CACHE Level 2 Diploma for Children's Care, Learning and Development (Northern Ireland). Retrieved from https://ncca.ie/media/6306/guidelines-for-good-practice.pdf, https://www.ncfe.org.uk/media/vnfj3ldn/603-4723-5-qualification-specification.pdf.

NCFE CACHE (2023a). Qualification Specification NCFE CACHE Level 2 Diploma for the Early Years Practitioner. Retrieved from https://www.ncfe.org.uk/media/emedws0k/603-3723-0-qualification-specification-version-2-0.pdf.

NCFE CACHE (2023b). Qualification specification NCFE CACHE Level 3 Diploma for the Early Years Workforce (Early Years Educator). Retrieved from https://www.ncfe.org.uk/media/ib1lta3p/601-2629-2-qualification-specification-version-5-8.pdf.

NCFE CACHE (2023d). Qualification Specification. NCFE CACHE Level 2 Diploma in Playwork QN: 610/0643/9. Retrieved from https://www.ncfe.org.uk/media/r0kfzymp/610-0643-9-qualification-specification-version-2-0.pdf.

NCFE CACHE (2023e). Qualification Specification: NCFE CACHE Level 3 Certificate in Understanding Playwork QN: 610/0644/0 NCFE CACHE Level 3 Diploma in Playwork QN: 610/0645/2. Retrieved from https://www.ncfe.org.uk/media/3phfqpnt/610-0644-0-and-610-0645-2-qualification-specification-version-1-2.pdf.

NCFE CACHE (2023f). Qualification Specification: NCFE CACHE Level 5 Diploma in Advanced Playwork (Wales) QN: 601/5370/2. Retrieved from https://www.ncfe.org.uk/media/pyolalyl/601-5370-2-qualification-specification-version-6-4.pdf.

NCFE CACHE (2024). Qualification Specification: NCFE CACHE Level 3 Award in Transition to Playwork QN: 603/7635/1. Retrieved from https://www.ncfe.org.uk/media/ta4e5tzn/603-7635-1-qualification-specification-version-1-3.pdf.

Neumann, E. A. (1971). The Elements of Play. New York: MSS Information Corporation.

Newstead, S. (2019). Le playwork à la recherche d'une identité perdue (Playwork – in search of an identity). Sciences du jeu. Retrieved from https://journals.openedition.org/sdj/2337

Nicholson, S. (1971). How NOT to Cheat Children: The Theory of Loose Parts. Landscape Architecture, 62, 30–34.

Normand, S., Soucisse, M. M., Melançon, M. P. V., Schneider, B. H., Lee, M. D., & Maisonneuve, M.-F. (2018). Observed Free-Play Patterns of Children With ADHD and Their Real-Life Friends. Journal of Abnormal Child Psychology, 47, 259–271.

Northern Ireland Curriculum (2007). The Northern Ireland Curriculum Primary. Retrieved from https://ccea.org.uk/downloads/docs/ccea-asset/Curriculum/The%20Northern%20Ireland%20Curriculum%20-%20Primary.pdf.

Nugent, B. (2024). Children and Young People's Views of Play: A Literature Review to Inform the Refresh of Scotland's Play Strategy 2024. Retrieved from https://www.playscotland.org/resources/print/Children-and-Young-Peoples-Views-of-Play-A-literature-review-to-inform-the-refresh-of-Scotlands-Play-Strategy-2024.pdf?plsctml_id=24685.

Odum, E. P. (1971). Fundamentals of Ecology. Philadelphia: W. B. Saunders Company.

## References

Office for Minister for Children (2004). READY, STEADY, PLAY! A National Play Policy. National Children's Office: Republic of Ireland.

Office for Minister for Children (2007). teenspace: National Recreation Policy for Young People. National Children's Office: Republic of Ireland.

Office of the First Minister and Deputy First Minister (2008). Play and Leisure Implementation Plan. Retrieved https://www.education-ni.gov.uk/sites/default/files/publications/education/play-and-leisure-policy-statement.pdf.

Office of the First Minister and Deputy First Minister (2011). Play and Leisure Implementation Plan: Narrative. Retrieved from https://www.education-ni.gov.uk/sites/default/files/publications/education/play-and-leisure-narrative.pdf. Office for First Minister and Deputy First Minister (2010). Play and Leisure in Northern Ireland – Your Right to Play. Retrieved February 9, 2013, from http://www.ofmdfmni.gov.uk/info_paper_chns_version_june_2009_final__2_.doc.

Palmer, S. (2003). Playwork as Reflective Practice. In F. Brown (Ed.) Playwork: Theory and Practice (pp. 176-190). Maidenhead: Open University Press.

Pardej, S. K., & Mayes, D. (2024). Prevalence and Correlates of Poor Safety Awareness and Accidental Injury in ASD, ADHD, ASD + ADHD, and Neurotypical Youth Samples. Journal of Autism and Developmental Studies, https://doi.org/10.1007/s10803-024-06417-z

NCFE CACHE (2023c). Qualification Specification: NCFE CACHE Level 3 Diploma for Children's Care, Learning and Development (Northern Ireland). Retrieved from https://www.ncfe.org.uk/media/jcdbfleo/603-6039-2-qualification-specification-version-1-4.pdf

Perasso, G., Camurati, G., Morrin, E., Dill, C., Dolidze, K., Clegg, T., Simonelli, Magione-Standish, A., Pansier, B., Gulyurtlu, S. C., Garone, A., & Rippen, H. (2021). Five Reasons Why Pediatric Settings Should Integrate the Play Specialist and Five Issues in Practice. Frontiers in Psychology, 12(68792), 1-5.

Pereira, J. V., Dionisio, J., Lopes, F., & Cordovil, R. (2023). Playing at the School Yard: "The Who's, the What's and the How Long's" of Loose Parts. Children, 10(240), 1-12.

Piaget, J. (1952). Play, Dreams and Imitation in Childhood. W.W. Norton & Co.

Play England (2009). Developing an adventure playground: the essential elements: Practice Scottish Qualifications Authority (SQA) (2018). Group Award Specification for: HNC Childhood Practice. Retrieved from https://www.sqa.org.uk/sqa/files_ccc/GroupAwardSpecificationGK9T15.pdf.

Play Wales (2022). Playwork Qualifications in Wales: For Playworkers and Others Who Work With Children. Retrieved from https://play.wales/wp-content/uploads/2023/03/Quals-booklet_2023.pdf.

Pollock, I., & Stewart, T. (2023). Professional Learning and the Reflective Practitioner. In M. Carroll & M. Wingrave (Eds.) Childhood Practice: A Reflective & Evidence-Based Approach (pp. 221-232). London: SAGE.

Power, S., Rhys, M., Taylor, C & Waldron, S. (2019). How Child-Centred Education Favours Some Learners More than Others. Review of Education, 7(3), 570-592.

Prieske, B., Withagen, R., Smith, Jl, & Zaal, F. T. J. M. (2015). Affordances in a Simple Playscape: Are Children Attracted to Challenging Affordances? Journal of Environmental Psychology, 41, 101-111.

Pyle, A., & Danniels, E. (2017) A Continuum of Play-Based Learning: The Role of the Teacher in Play-Based Pedagogy and the Fear of Hijacking Play, Early Education and Development, 28(3), 274-289.

Quaintrell, Y. (2021). Playwork in Prisons: an Exploratory Case Study. In P. King & S. Newstead (Eds.) Further Perspectives on Researching Play from a Playwork Perspective (pp. 9-19). London: Routledge.

Quennerstedt, A., Robinson, C., & l'Anson, J. (2018). The UNCRC: The Voice of Global Consensus on Children's Rights? Nordic Journal of Human Rights, 36:1, 38-54, DOI: 10.1080/18918131.2018.1453589.

Reed, M., & Canning, N. (2010). Reflective Practice in the Early Years. London: SAGE.

Rennie, S. (2003). Making Play Work: the Fundamental Role of Play in the Development of Social Relationship Skills. In F. Brown (Ed.) Playwork Theory and Practice (pp. 32-48). Maidenhead: Open University Press.

Rico, A. P., & Janot, J. B. (2021). Children's Right to Play and Its Implementation: A Comparative, International Perspective. Journal of New Approaches in Education Research, 10, 297-294.

Ridgers, N. D., Knowles, Z. R., & Sayers, J. (2012) Encouraging Play in the Natural Environment: a Child-Focused Case Study of Forest School, Children's Geographies, 10:1, 49-65, DOI: 10.1080/14733285.2011.638176.

Rothlein, L., & Brett, A. (1987). Children's Teachers', and Parents' Perceptions of Play. Early Childhood Research Quarterly, 2, 45-53.

Rubin, K. H. (2001). Play Observation Scale (POS). University of Maryland Center for Children, Relationships and Culture. Retrieved from http://www.rubin-lab.umd.edu/Coding%20Schemes/POS%20Coding%20Scheme%202001.pdf.

Russell, W. (2012). 'I Get Such a Feeling Out Of... Those moments': Playwork, Passion, Politics and Space. International Journal of Play, 1(1), 51-63.

Ryan, V., (1999). Developmental Delay, Symbolic Play and Non-Directive Play Therapy. Clinical Child Psychology and Psychiatry, 4(2), 167-185.

Ryan, V. (2004). Adapting Non-Directive Play Therapy for Children With Attachment Disorders. Clinical Child Psychology and Psychiatry, 9(1), 75-87.

Salmi, W. N., & Hanson, V. F. (2021). Effectiveness of Hospital Play Interventions Program in Reducing Anxiety and Negative Emotions Among Hospitalized Children in Ras Al-Khaimah, United Arab Emirates. International Journal of Nursing Science Practice and Research, 7(2), 41-50.

Sandseter, E. B. H. (2009a). Characteristics of Risky Play. Journal of Adventure Education and Outdoor Learning, 9(1), 3-21.

Sandseter, E. B. H. (2009b). Risk Play and Risk Management in Norwegian Preschools- A Qualitative Observational Study. Safety Science Monitor, 1(2), 1-12.

Sandseter, E. B. H., Storli, R., & Sando, O. J. (2022). The Relationship between Indoor Environments and children's Play - Confined Spaces and Materials, Education, 3-13, DOI: 10.1080/03004279.2020.1869798

Sawyers, J. K. (1994). The Presachool Playground: Developing Skills Through Outdoor Play. Journal of Physical Education, Recreation & Dance, 65(6), 31-33.

Schön, D. A. (1983). The Reflective Practitioner: How Professionals Think in Action. London: Temple Smith.

Scotland, P., & Elsley, S. (2020). Progress Review of Scotland's Play Strategy (2020). Retrieved from https://www.playscotland.org/resources/print/Play-Scotland-Play-Strategy-Review-2020.pdf?plsctml_id=20940.

Scotland, P., & Elsley, S. (2021). Progress Review of Scotland's Play Strategy 2021: Play in a COVID-19 context. Retrieved from https://www.playscotland.org/resources/print/Play-Scotland-Play-Strategy-Review-Play-in-Covid-2021.pdf?plsctml_id=20943.

Scott, E., & Panksepp, J. (2003). Rough-and-Tumble Play in Human Children. Aggressive Behavior, 29, 539-551.

Scottish Government (2013a). Play Strategy for Scotland: Our Vision. Edinburgh: Scottish Government. Retrieved June 28, 2013, from http://www.scotland.gov.uk/Resource/0042/00425722.pdf.

Scottish Government (2013b). Play Strategy for Scotland: Our Action Plan. Retrieved from https://www.gov.scot/binaries/content/documents/govscot/publications/strategy-plan/2013/10/play-strategy-scotland-action-plan/documents/00437132-pdf/00437132-pdf/govscot%3Adocument.

Scottish Government (2017). Health and Social Care Standards: My support, my life. Retrieved from https://hub.careinspectorate.com/media/2544/sg-health-and-social-care-standards.pdf.

Scottish Qualifications (2021a). Scottish Vocational Qualification 2: Social Services (Children and Young People) at SCQF level 6. Authority Retrieved from https://secure.sqa.org.uk/sqa/files_ccc/Information%20Sheet%20SSCYP%20Level%202.pdf.

Scottish Qualifications Authority (2021b). Scottish Vocational Qualification 3: Social Services (Children and Young People) at SCQF level 7. Retrieved from https://secure.sqa.org.uk/sqa/files_ccc/Information_Sheet_SSCYP_level3.pdf.

Scottish Qualifications Authority (SQA) (2024). SVQ's in Playwork. Retrieved from https://www.sqa.org.uk/sqa/90600.html.

Scottish Social Services Council (2024). Codes of Practice for Social Service Workers and Employers. Retrieved from https://news.sssc.uk.com/news/your-new-sssc-codes-of-practice.

Shamsudin, I. D. (2021). Child-Led Play for Children With Autism Spectrum Disorder (ASD): Lessons Learned from Parents. Jurnal Pendidkan Bitara UPSI, 14(1), 44-53.

Sidhu, J., Barlas, N., & Lifter, K. (2022). On the Meanings of Functional Play: A Review and Clarification of Definitions. Topics in Early Childhood Special Education, 42(2), 189-201.

Slotkin, J. S. (1950). Social Anthropology: The Science of Human Society and Culture. New York: The Macmillan Company.

Smilansky, S. (1968). The Effects of Sociodramatic Play on Disadvantaged Pre-School Children. New York: John Wiley & Sons Inc.

Smith, P., & St. George, J. M. (2023). Play Fighting (rough-and-Tumble Play) in Children: Developmental and Evolutionary Perspectives. International Journal of Play, 12(1), 113-126.

## References

Smith, P. K., & Vollstedt, R. (1985). On Defining Play: An Empirical Study of the Relationship between Play and Various Play Criteria. Child Development, 56(4), 1042-1050.

Smith-Gilman, S. (2018). The Arts, Loose Parts and Conversations. Journal of the Canadian Association for Curriculum Studies, 16(1), 90-103.

Smtih, S. (2018). Understanding of Play for Children With Profound and Multiple Learning Disabilities (PMLD). In W. Russell, S. Lester & H. Smith (Eds.) Practice-Based Research in Children's Play (pp. 187-202). Bristol: Policy Press.

Social Care Wales (2018). All Wales Induction Framework for Early Years and Childcare Introduction and Guidance. Retrieved from https://socialcare.wales/cms-assets/documents/All-Wales-induction-framework-for-early-years-and-childcare.pdf

Social Care Wales (2022). Children's Care, Learning, and Development National Occupational Standards. Retrieved from https://socialcare.wales/resources-guidance/early-years-and-childcare/national-occupational-standards-nos/childrens-care-learning-and-development.

Spencer, R. A., Joshi, N., Branje, K., McIsaac, J.-L. D., Cawley, J., Rehman, L., Kirk, S. F. L., & Stone, M., (2019). Educator Perceptions on the Benefits and Challenges of Loose Parts Play in the Outdoor Environments of Childcare Centres. Public Health, 6(4), 461-476.

Stahmer, A. C. (1995). Teaching Symbolic Play Skills to Children with Autism Using Pivotal Response Training. Journal of Autism and Developmental Disorders, 25(2), 123-141.

Stephen, C., & Plowman, L. (2014) Digital play. In L. Brooker, M. Blaise & S. Edwards (Eds.) Sage Handbook of Play and Learning in Early Childhood (pp. 330-341). London: Sage.

Stobart, T.(Ed.) ( (1998). Take 10 for Play Playwork Training Course. Gloucestershire: University of Gloucestershire.

Stordal, G., Follow, G., & Pareliussen, I. (2015). Betwixt the Wild, Unknown and the Safe: Play and the Affordances of Nature. International Journal of Early Childhood Environmental Education, 3(1), 28-37.

Storli, R., & Hagen, T. L. (2010) Affordances in Outdoor Environments and Children's Physically Active Play in Pre-School, European Early Childhood Education Research Journal, 18(4), 445-456, DOI: 10.1080/1350293X.2010.525923

Sturrock, G. (1999). The Impossible Science of the Unique Being. In P. Else & G. Sturrock (Eds.) Therapeutic Playwork Reader One 1995-2000 (pp. 122-130). Eastleigh: Common Threads Publications.

Sturrock, G. (2003). The Ludic Third. In P. Else & G. Sturrock (Eds.) Therapeutic Playwork Reader Two 2000-2005 (pp. 28-37). Sheffield: Lumos.

Sturrock, G., & Else, p (1998). 'The Colorado Paper'–The Playground as Therapeutic Space: Playwork as Healing. In G. Sturrock & P. Else (Eds.) Therapeutic Playwork Reader One 1995-2000 (pp. 73-104).

Sturrock, G., Russell, W., & Else, P. (2004). Towards Ludogogy: Parts I, II and III. In P. Else & G. Sturrock (Eds.) Therapeutic Playwork Reader Two 2000-2005 (pp. 60-95). Oxford: Oxford Play Association.

Sutton-Smith, B. (1997). The Ambiguity of Play. USA: Havard.

Taylor, M. E., & Boyer, W. (2020). Play-Based Learning: Evidence-Based Research to Improve Children's Learning Experiences in the Kindergarten Classroom. Early Childhood Education Journal, 48, 127-133. https://doi.org/10.1007/s10643-019-00989-7.

Toub, T. S., Rajan, V., Golinkoff, R. M., & Hirsh-Pasek, K. (2016). Guided Play: A Solution to the Play Versus Discovery Learning Dichotomy. In D. C. Geary & D. B. Berch (Eds.), Evolutionary Perspectives on Child Development and Education (pp. 117-141). Springer International Publishing/Springer Nature. https://doi.org/10.1007/978-3-319-29986-0_5.

TUSLA (2024). A Guide to Inspection in Early Years Services Retrieved from https://www.tusla.ie/uploads/content/EYI-GDE12.2_EYI_Guide_to_Early_Years_Inspections_FINAL_.pdf.

UK Commission for Employment and Skills (2011). National Occupational Standards Quality Criteria with Explanatory Notes. Retrieved from https://assets.publishing.service.gov.uk/media/5a7e32d740f0b62302689cd1/nos-quality-criteria-2011.pdf

United Nations (2013). General Comment No. 17 (2013) on the Right of the Child to Rest, Leisure, Play, Recreational Activities, Cultural Life and the Arts (art. 31). Retrieved from https://digitallibrary.un.org/record/778539?ln=en&v=pdf.

United Nations International Children's Emergency Fund (UNICEF) (2019). A summary of the UN Convention on the Rights of the Child. Retrieved from https://www.unicef.org.uk/wp-content/uploads/2019/10/UNCRC_summary-1_1.pdf.

Usher, W. (2010). Creating Sensory Play At Little or No Cost. Milton Keynes: The Play Doctors.

Vaisarova, J., & Reynolds, A. J. (2022). Is More Child-Initiated Always Better? Exploring Relations between Child-Initiated Instruction and preschoolers' School Readiness. Educational Assessment, Evaluation and Accountability, 24, 195-226. https://doi.org/10.1007/s11092-021-09376-6.

Vickerius, M., & Sandberg, A. (2004). The Significance of Play and the Environment Around Play. Early Child Development and Care, 176:2, 207-217, DOI: 10.1080/0300443042000319430.

Voce, A. (2015). Policy for Play: Responding to Children's Forgotten Right. Bristol: Policy Press.

von Uexküll, J. (1982). The Theory of Meaning.

Vygotsky, L. (1978). Mind in Society: Development of Higher Psychological Processes. Cambridge: Harvard University Press.

Warash, B. G., Root, A. E., & Doris, M. D. (2019). Parents' Perceptions of Play: a Comparative Study of Spousal Perspectives. In J. M. Nicholson & D. B. Wisneski (Eds.) Reconsidering The Role of Play in Early Childhood (pp. 242-250). London: Routledge.

Wardle, F. (2000). Supporting Constructive Play in the Wild–Guidelines for Learning Outdoors. Child Care Information Exchange, 133, 26-30.

Webster, A. (2000). The Facilitating Role of the Play Specialist. Paediatric Nursing, 12(7), 24-27.

Weisberg, D. S., Hirsh-Pasek, K., & Golinkoff, R. M. (2013). Guided Play: Where Curricular Goals Meet a Playful Pedagogy. Mind, Brain, and Education, 7(2), 104-112.

Welsh Assembly Government (2002). A Play Policy for Wales. Cardiff: National Assembly for Wales.

Welsh Assembly Government (2006). Play Policy Implementation Plan. Cardiff: National Assembly for Wales.

Welsh Government (2012). National Minimum Standards for Regulated Child Care. Retrieved from https://dera.ioe.ac.uk/14202/7/120309regchildcareen_Redacted.pdf.

Welsh Government (2014). Wales – a Play Friendly Country: Statutory Guidance. Cardiff: Welsh Government.

Welsh Government (2019). Review of the National Minimum Standards for Regulated Childcare. Retrieved from https://gov.wales/sites/default/files/publications/2019-08/review-of-the-national-minimum-standards-for-regulated-childcare.pdf.

Welsh Government (2022). A Curriculum for Funded Non-Maintained Nursery Settings. Cardiff: Welsh Government.

Welsh Government (2023). National Minimum Standards for Regulated Childcare for Children Up to the Age of 12 Years. Retrieved from https://www.gov.wales/sites/default/files/publications/2023-11/national-minimum-standards-for-regulated-childcare_0.pdf

Wenger, E. (1998). Communities of Practice: Learning, Meaning, and Identity. Cambridge: Cambridge University Press.

Whitebread, D., Basilio, M., Kuvalja, M., & Verma, M. (2012). The Importance of Play: A Report on the Value of Children's Play with a Series of Policy Recommendations. Retrieved from https://www.csap.cam.ac.uk/media/uploads/files/1/david-whitebread---importance-of-play-report.pdf

Willans, B. (2021). Using Playwork Perspectives and Ethnographic Research to Move Towards an Understanding of Autistic Play Culture. In P. King & S. Newstead (Eds.) Further Perspectives on Researching Play From A Playwork Perspective (pp. 20-36). London: Routledge.

Wing, L., & Gould, J. (1979). Severe Impairments of Social Interaction and Associated Abnormalities in Children: Epidemiology and Classification. Journal of Autism and Developmental Disorders, 9, 11-29.

Wiseman, K.V., McArdell, L.E., Bottini, S.B. et al. A Meta-Analysis of Safety Skill Interventions for Children, Adolescents, and Young Adults with Autism Spectrum Disorder. Rev J Autism Dev Disord 4, 39-49 (2017). https://doi.org/10.1007/s40489-016-0096-7

Wood, D. (1988). How Children Think and Learn: The Social Contexts of Cognitive Development, Second Edition. Oxford: Blackwell.

Wood, D. J., Bruner, J. S., & Ross, G. (1976). The Role of Tutoring in Problem-Solving. Journal of Child Psychology and Psychiatry, 17(2), 89-100.

Wood, E. (2013). Play, Learning and the Early Childhood Curriculum 3rd Edition. London: SAGE.

Wood, E. (2022). Play and Learning in Early Childhood Education: Tensions and Challenges. Child Studies, (1), 15-26. https://doi.org/10.21814/childstudies.4124.

Wood, E., & Bennett, N. (1998). Teachers' Theories of Play: Constructivist or Social Constructivist?, Early Child Development and Care, 140:1, 17-30, DOI:10.1080/0300443981400103.

Woodall, J., & Kinsella, K. (2017). Playwork in Prison as a Mechanism to Support Family Health and Well-Being. Health Education Journal, 76(7), 842-852.

Woods, A. (Ed.) (2017). Child-Initiated Play and Learning: Planning for Possibilities in the Early Years. London: Routledge.

Woolley, H., & Lowe, A. (2013) Exploring the Relationship between Design Approach and Play Value of Outdoor Play Spaces, Landscape Research, 38(1), 53–74. DOI: 10.1080/01426397.2011.640432.

Zachariou, A., & Whitebread, D. (2015) Musical Play and Selfregulation: Does Musical Play Allow for the Emergence of Self-Regulatory Behaviours? International Journal of Play, 4(2), 116–135, DOI: 10.1080/21594937.2015.1060572.

# INDEX

Acer, Dilek 25
active engagement 3; see also criteria of play
adult: led 28-30, 35, 38, 41-42, 76, 80-84
 (see also play);
passive role 35-37, 39, 41, 43, 47, 62-63, 76 (see also Adult Intervention Style); practitioner 11, 34, 39; role 11, 14, 18, 25, 31, 35, 40-42, 45-47, 56, 77 (see also Adult Intervention Style)
Adult Intervention Style (AIS) xv, 10-11, 13-14, 35-40, 45-48, 51, 57, 62, 73, 75-76, 78, 80
adulteration 11-12, 18, 35, 51, 56-57, 62; see also play cycle
Adventure Playground (AP) 4-5, 15, 18, 38, 84; see also junk, playground
affordances 6, 10, 11, 13, 15, 17, 18, 19, 20, 25; emotional 17; functional 17; perceived 18; potential 17-18; social 17; structural 17; see also Gibson, James J.
After-School Club (ASC) 1, 4-5, 15, 18, 22, 33, 36-37, 72, 84
Agored 73-74; Level 2 Award in Playwork Practice 73-74; Level 2 Certificate in Playwork Principles into Practice (P3) (Wales) 73-74; Level 3 Diploma in Playwork Principles into Practice (P3) (Wales) 73-74; see also qualifications, vocational
Aistear 40; see also curriculum
Allen of Hurtwood, Lady Marjorie 22
Amani, Jaquiline 27
Andreasson, Filippa 27
Ashton, Kate 31
Aslan, Büşra 25
Article 31 6, 26-27, 33-34, 65-68, 75, 79; see also United Nations, Convention on the Rights of the Child

Atkins, Ladonna 4, 42, 63
Attention Deficit Hyperactivity Disorder (ADHD) 25, 29-30, 33; see also atypicality
atypicality 25, 29-30, 33, 45
Autism 25, 29, 30, 33; see also atypicality
Autonomy 27, 32, 34
Axline, Virginia 6, 30; see also play therapy (PT); non-directive
Aytekin, Aynur 5

Backman, Anna 27
Baines, Ed 5
Ball, David 32, 34
Barlas, Natasha 23
Barrouillet, Pierre 3
Basilio, Marisol 6, 24
Bateson, Gregory 10
Benjamin, Joe 22
Bentley, Arthur F. 45
Bergen, Doris 6, 28, 41, 81
BIG Lottery funding 2
Bishop, Julia 18, 24
Black, Elizabeth 40, 83
Blatchford, Peter 5
Bogunovich, Jessica 20
Boutall, Trevor 72
Branje, Karina 20-21
Brett, Arlene 84
Bronfenbrenner, Urie 81; see also theory, ecological systems
Bruner, Jerome S. 3, 40
Brussoni, Mariana 33
Bullerby 18; see also Kyttä, Marketta
Burr, Brandon 4, 42, 63
Bulut, Okan 21

Çakırer, H. Billur 25
Cameron, Ashley D. 63
Campbell-Barr, Verity 26-27, 81
Cankaya, Ozlem 21
Cannarella, Amanda M. 63
Canning, Natalie 27, 43, 63
Care Inspectorate (CI) (Scotland) 69; *see also* Regulation and Inspection
Care Inspectorate of Wales (CIW) 69; *see also* Regulation and Inspection
Care Standards Act 2000 69-69; *see also* legislation
Carmarthenshire Association of Voluntary Services (CAVS) 2
Carroll, Geoff 72
Casey, Theresa 21
Casper, Rachel 30
Cawley, Jane 20-21
Çelebi, Arzu, 5
Çelebioğlu, Ayda 5
cell 18; *see also* Kyttä, Marketta
challenges 33, 80-82
Cheung, Rebecca H. P. 27
child: centered 6, 40; directed 6, 14, 26-28, 40-42, 47, 73 (*see also* play-based, learning); initiated 6, 27-28; led 2, 4, 6, 14, 21, 25-34, 41, 44, 46, 65, 73, 76, 80-81, 84
Child and Family Agency Act 2013 (Republic of Ireland) 70; *see also* legislation
childcare 2, 6, 10, 13-14, 20, 43, 70, 80; centre 71; Child Care Act 1991 (Early Years Services) Regulations (Republic of Ireland) 70-71; (*see also* legislation); facility 67; inspection 70; practice 13; provider 67; provision 43, 65, 68-70; qualification 72-73, 83; register 69; setting 4, 37, 67-70; workers 2, 6, 7, 9, 12-13, 22, 29, 31, 33, 37, 39-40, 45, 47, 72, 84-85
Child Minding and Day Care (Wales) Order 2016 69; *see also* legislation
Child Minding and Day Care (Wales) Regulations 2002 69; *see also* legislation
childminding 68-70
Childminding and Day Care for Children Under Age 12: Minimum Standards (Northern Ireland) 69; *see also* National, Minimum Standards
Children Act 1989 68-69; *see also* legislation

Children Act 2004 68; *see also* legislation
Children Act 2006 68; *see also* legislation
Children (Scotland) Act 1995 68; *see also* legislation
Children (NI) Order 1995: Guidance and Regulations Volume 2 Family Support, Child Minding, and Day Care 68-69; *see also* legislation
choice: affordances 18; free 3, 66; play 2, 4, 27-28, 32, 66, 68, 75, 81-82; *see also* criteria of play
City & Guilds (C&G): Level 2 Diploma for the Early Years Practitioner (England) 72, 74; Level 2 Diploma in Children's Care, Learning and Development (Northern Ireland); Level 3 Diploma in Children's Care, Learning and Development (Northern Ireland); Level 3 Early Years Practitioner (Early Years Educator) (England) 72, 74; *see also* qualifications, vocational
City & Guilds/WJEC: Level 2 Children's Care, Play, Learning and Development: Core (Wales) 72, 74; Level 2 Children's Care, Play, Learning and Development: Practice (Wales) 72, 74; Level 2 Children's Care, Play, Learning and Development: Practice and Theory (Wales) 72, 74; Level 3 Children's Care, Play, Learning and Development: Practice (Wales) 72, 74; Level 3 Children's Care, Play, Learning and Development: Practice and Theory (Wales) 72, 74; Level 4 Preparing for Leadership and Management in Children's Care, Play, Learning and Development (Wales) 72, 74; Level 4 Professional Practice in Children's Care, Play, Learning and Development (Wales) 72, 74; *see also* qualifications, vocational
Clement, Jennifer 28
closed access 5
Cogher, Lesley 30
Cognitive Development Theory (CDT) 3
'Colorado Paper' 1, 8-9, 13, 84-85; *see also* Else, Perry; Sturrock, Gordon
collaborative play 35, 41-42, 47, 80-81; *see also* play-based, continuum; play-based, learning
complex intervention 6, 11, 14, 18, 35, 36, 38, 39, 41, 42, 43, 47, 56, 62, 76, 80; *see also* Adult Intervention Style

common threads xiv, 71
Community of Practice (CoP) 43
concepts 21-22, 27; *see also* play, menu
Conn, Carmel 25, 29
containing role 12, 35, 39
continuing professional development (CPD) 2
continuum of play 41
Cooper, Paul 29
Cordovil, Rita 20-21
Cornell, Megan 20-21
Costall, Alan 17
Council for the Awards in Care, Health and Education (CACHE) 72-74
Cranwell, Keith 22
Crowley, Kevin 4, 84
criteria of play 3-4, 24
Csikszentmihalyi, Mihaly 10, 13; *see also* flow
curriculum: Aistear: The Early Childhood Curriculum Framework (Republic or Ireland) 40; Early Years Foundation Phase (FP) (Wales) 40; Early Years Foundation Stage (EYFS) (England) 40; for Wales (Wales) 40; Northern Ireland Curriculum Primary (Northern Ireland) 40
customised qualifications 71, 73
Cutter-Mackenzie, Amy 81

Danniels, Erica 5-6, 35, 41, 47
day care 5, 62, 68-70
de Water, Erik 25
Dekkers, Tycho J. 25
Delicâte, Nicola 33
Department for Education (DfE) (UK Government) 69, 72; *see also* legislation
Department for Education and Employment (DfEE) (UK Government) 1; *see also* legislation
Department of Health and Social Services (DoHSS) (Northern Ireland) 70; *see also* legislation
development 70-71, 75, 77, 81-84
Developmental Play Assessment (DPA) 63; *see also* observation
Dewey, John 45
Dietze, Beverlie 20-21
Dionisio, Jadiane 20-21
Disability 29; *see also* atypicality

Dodd, Helen F. 6, 32
Doris, Meghan D. 84
Downes, Graham 5
Dysplay 30; *see also* the play cycle

Early Childhood Education Centres (ECEC) 25
early years: education xiv, 4, 10, 20, 81, 83; Foundation Phase (EYFP) (Wales) 40 (*see also* legislation); Foundation Stage (EYFS) (England) 40, 69, 72 (*see also* legislation); Foundation Stage Framework (EYFSF) (England) 72 (*see also* legislation); Inspectorate (Republic of Ireland) 70; National Occupational Standards (NOS) 73; practice 31; practitioner xv, 40, 84; provider 67, 72; qualification 72, 74; register 68-69; registration 70; settings xv, 81; TULSA 70, 83; worker 31, 33, 43, 85
ecological: perspective 16; principles 15; systems theory (EST) 81, exo-system 81, macro-system 81, micro-system 81, meso-system 81 (*see also* Bronfenbrenner, Urie)
Edwards, Gail, 43
Edwards, Susan 81
effector 17; *see also* environment, functional cycle
elements: of Community of Practice 43; natural 19, 22; of play-based learning 40; of play criteria 4; of play cycle 4, 6, 8-11, 13-14, 35, 48, 63, 77, 80, 83; of play menu 21-22; of potential challenge 84; of risky play 3, 24, 33; of socio-dramatic play 24
Else, Perry xiii, 1, 6, 8-11, 13, 15, 30-31, 35, 39, 41, 46, 80, 84-85; *see also* 'Colorado Paper'
empowerment 27, 63
environment: affordances 17-18, 25; child-friendly 66; external xiv; emotional 16-17; functional cycle 16-17, 25, 33; indoor 18-19, 25, 71, 76; inner world 16; inspection framework 69; loose parts 20, 23, 37; ludic ecology 16; natural 19, 69-70; object 16-17, 23-24, 51; objective 16; outdoor 18-19, 33, 71, 76; outer world 16; physical 16-17, 19, 70-71; play xv, 1, 4, 6, 13-19, 21, 24-25, 60, 66, 70-71, 73, 75-76, 78, 80, 85; playwork xv; relaxed 5; resource 19, 21, 25, 28, 45, 60; safe 66; sand 23; senses 19, 22; social 16-17, 22; support 85

established play cycle 4, 10-12, 14, 22, 35, 37-39, 48, 50-63; see also play cycle
external: environment xiv; goal 3-4, 27-28, 41, 79; objects 10-11, 16; perceptual cue 10-12, 21; world 4, 12, 15, 21
external perceptual 10-12, 21; see also environment, functional cycle

Fahy, Sarah 33
Family and Children Measures (Wales) 2010 66; see also legislation
Fields: of Constrained Action (FCA) 18; of Free Action (FFA) 15, 18; of Promoted Action (FPA) 18; see also Kyttä, Marketta
Fisher, Kelly R. 84
First, Zehra S. 25
FitzGibbon, Lily 32
Flannigan, Caileigh 20-21
Follo, Gro 18, 27
Forest Schools (FS) 5, 13, 19-20
Frame Analysis 10
functional: affordances 17; cycle 10-11, 13-17, 25 (see also von Uexküll, Jakob); play 18, 23, 25
Fung, Sally 31
Fussy, Daniel S. 27

Garcia, Isabel G. 25
Garden, Angela 5
General Comment 17 26, 65; see also Article 31
Gentile, Axel D. 27
Gibbs, Graham 43-45
Gibson, James J. 6, 10-11, 13, 15, 17, 25; see also affordances
Gibson, Jenny L. 20-21
Gill, Tim 20-21, 34
Glasshouse 18; see also Kyttä, Marketta
Goffman, Erving 10
Goldstein, Suzanne L. 20
Golinkoff, Roberta M. 27, 84
Gould, Judith 29
Gözen, Göksu 25
Government: England 78; Northern Ireland 27, 65, 80, 82; Polish 26; Republic of Ireland 27, 65-66, 80, 82; Scottish 3, 27, 65-67, 69, 80, 82; United Kingdom (UK) 26, 65, 67; Welsh 3, 5, 27-28, 34, 40, 65-66, 69, 80, 82; Welsh Assembly 27-28, 34, 65-66

Great Ormand Street Hospital (GOSH) 5
Grof, Stanislav 8
Gross, Karl 3
Gryfe, Shelly G. 84
Gull, Carla 20

Haiat, Hana 5
Hall, Granville S. 3
Hanson, Victoria F. 5
Hateli, Bahare 30
Health and Safety Executive (HSE) 32-34
Health and Social Care: Services 70; Standards (Scotland) 69-70; Trusts (Northern Ireland) 69
Hébert, Cristyne 44
Hebron, Judith 30
Heft, Harry 17
Higher National Certificate (HNC) Level 9 Childhood Practice (Scotland) 73-74; see also qualifications, vocational
Hirsh-Pasek, Kathy 27
Holiday Playscheme (HPS) 4-5, 18, 72, 74
Holloway, Sarah L. 4
Homeyer, Linda E. 30
hospital 5, 67, 69, 80, 85
Houser, Natalie E. 20-21
Howard, Justine 3-4, 17, 29, 40, 47, 81, 84
Hughes, Bob 3, 21, 23-24
Hughes, Leslie 29
Hyvönen, Pirkko 17, 84
hypothetical definition of play 4, 80; see also play, definition

identity 21-22, 83; see also play, menu
Iivonen, Susanna 23
inner world 9-10, 12, 15-16, 78, 85
International Play Association (IPA) 1, 8
intrinsic motivation 3-4, 27-28, 79; see also criteria of play
Irish Statute Book (ISB) (Republic of Ireland) 70

Josefi, Orit 30
Joshi, Nila 20-21
Jun-Tai, Norma 5
Jung, Carl G. 9
junk: material 42; modelling 31, 38, 42; playground 22; see also Adventure Playground
Juujärvi, Marjaana 17

knowledge, skills and understanding (K) 1-73, 75-78, 80, 83-84; *see also* qualifications, vocational
Kaivola, Taina 18-19
Kalyva, Efrosini 30
Kefeli, Hatice 25
King, Pete 2, 4-6, 8-14, 17, 22, 25, 30-31, 34-35, 40-42, 44, 46-48, 63, 80-84
Kinsella, Karina 5
Kirk, Sara F. L. 20-21
Kleppe, Rasmus 33
Klintwall, Lars 27
Knowles, Zoe R. 19
Kolen, Angela M. 21
Koukourikos, Konstantinos 5
Krason, Katarzyna 30
Krasnor, Linda R. 3
Küçükoğlu, Sibel 5
Kuvalja, Martina 6, 24, 25
Kyratzis, Amy 18
Kyttä, Marketta 15, 17-18, 25

Laaksoharju, Taina 18
L'Anson, John 26
Leach, Jamie 21
learning xiv, xv, 5-7, 27-29, 31, 35, 40-41, 43, 66, 69-70, 72-76, 78, 81-84; *see also* play-based, learning
learning outcomes (LO) 27, 72-73, 75-78, 83; *see also* qualifications, vocational
Lee, Matthew D. 25, 30
Lefebvre, Henri 16
legislation xiv, 6, 68-69, 71, 80-82, 84
legislation.gov.uk 66, 68-69
Lester, Kathryn J. 6, 32
levels of hierarchy xv, 10-11, 14, 18, 35-36, 39, 42, 47, 56-57; *see also* Adult Intervention Styles
Lifta, Karin 23, 63
Lindon, Jenni 28, 43
Loebach, Janet 26
loop and flow 9; *see also* play cycle
loose parts 4, 6, 10-11, 13, 15, 20-25, 31, 37, 76-77, 80; *see also* play types, loose parts play
Lopes, Frederico 20-21
Lowe, Alison 15
ludic ecology 8, 15
Lynch, Helen 33

Mackley, Honar 20-21
Maisonneuve, Marie-France 25, 30
Marsh, Jackie 18, 24
Mason, Emanuel J. 63
Mayes, Susan D. 33
Maynard, Trisha 5, 28
McIsaac, Jessie-Lee D. 20-21
McKendrick, John H. 26
meaning: carrier 16-17; receiver 16-17; *see also* environment, functional cycle
medial intervention 6, 11, 14, 18, 35-36, 38-43, 47, 56, 62, 76, 80; *see also* Adult Intervention Style
Melançon, Marie P. 25, 30
Melhuish, Edward 33
meta-lude 9; *see also* play cycle
Miles, Gareth 4, 81, 84
Mobile Play Provision (MPP) 5
Morrison, M. O. 30
Mugford, Eleanor 60

National: Certificate 73; charity 5; Children's Office 66, 82; Council for Curriculum and Assessment (NCCA) 40 (*see also* curriculum); Council for Further Education (NCFE) 71-74 (*see also* qualifications, vocational); Minimum Standards 43, 65, 69, 78, 82; NCFE CACHE 72-74; NCFE PARS 71, 73; Occupational Standards 9, 43, 65, 80; Playing Fields Association 3, 15; Play Policy 66; Recreation Policy 66; strategy 66
Nesbit, Rachel J. 6, 32
Neumann, Eva, A. 4, 80
Newstead, Shelly xiii
Nicholson, Simon 6, 11, 13, 20-21, 25, 80
non-: digital 24; directive (*see also* play therapy); directive play 6, 26, 30-32, 34; directive play practice (NDPP) 31; Directive Play Therapy (NDPT) 30; gendered 21; human 49-52, 54-56, 58, 61-62, 87; (*see also* Play Cycle Observation Method (PCOM)); literal 3 (*see also* criteria of play); maintained nurseries 41; physical 10; play 75; target child 49-62, 87 (*see also* Play Cycle Observation Method (PCOM)); verbal 9, 28-29, 57, 62, 76
Normand, Sébastien 25, 30
Nugent, Briege 66
nurseries xiv, xv, 5, 25, 41, 66, 85

observation xv, 2, 4, 6, 13-14, 24, 31, 35, 45-48, 51-64, 73, 75-78, 80, 86-87; see also Play Cycle Observation Method (PCOM)
Odum, Eugene P. 16
Office: Education and Standards (Ofsted) 69; for First Minister and Deputy First Minister (OFMDFM) (Northern Ireland) 27, 65, 67, 80, 82; of Law Reform 70; for Minister for Children (OMC) (Republic of Ireland) 27, 66, 80, 82; for Standards in Education (OfSted) 68 (see also Regulation and Inspection)
Olsen, Lise L. 33
open access 5; see also play
outcome: adult-led 28-29; developmental 84; educational 84; learning 27, 70, 72, 76-77; National Occupational Standards (NOS) 72; play 3-4, 27, 47, 70, 82
outer world 9-10, 16-17
Out of School Club (OOSC) 1, 4

Palmer, Sue 43-44
Panksepp, Jaak 32
Pantelidou, Parthenopi 5
Pareliussen, Ingar 18, 27
Pardej, Sara K. 33
participation 26, 76; see also United Nations, Convention on the Rights of the Child
Pepler, Debra J. 3
Pereira, Joana V. 20-21
performance criteria 72-73, 75-78, 80, 82; see also qualifications, vocational
person-centered 30
Piaget, Jean 3, 24; see also Cognitive Development Theory
Pike, Ian 33
Pimlott-Wilson, Helena 4
Planning (Scotland) Act 2019 66
play: activities 24, 36, 38, 41, 42, 46, 51, 81, 83; adult-led 28-30, 35, 41-42, 76, 80-84; choice 2-4, 18, 27, 32, 66, 68, 75, 78, 81-82; collaborative 35, 41-42, 47, 80-81; content 8, 17, 27-28, 68; context xv, 3-5, 24, 26, 31, 34, 36, 42-43, 47, 67, 80-85; control 4, 11, 18, 22, 27-28, 32, 34-35, 38, 41, 45, 51, 56-57, 62, 68, 76, 80-83; definition of 2-4, 6, 9-10, 13, 23, 27-28, 41, 71, 80, 82-84; directed 4, 6, 14, 26-28, 31, 41, 47, 65, 70, 73; fate 83 (see also rhetoric); free 23, 28, 39, 41, 81 (see also continuum); freely chosen 2-4, 27-28, 65, 70-71, 76, 79, 82, 84 (see also definition of play); frivolous activity 83 (see also rhetoric); guided 27, 41 (see also play-based, learning); hospital 5, 67, 80, 85; identity 21-22, 83 (see also play, menu; rhetoric); imaginary 93 (see also rhetoric); inquiry 41; intrinsically motivated 3-4, 27-28, 79 (see also play, definition of); menu 21-22 (see also Bob Hughes); no external goal 3-4, 27-28, 79 (see also play, definition of); outcomes 4, 40, 67, 75, 78, 81-84; power 32, 83-84 (see also rhetorics); practice 3-6, 31, 34, 67; process xv, 27, 31, 46; progress (rhetoric) 83-84; resource 2, 11, 13, 24-25, 31, 37, 39, 42, 45, 51-52, 56, 60, 62, 67, 71, 73, 75-78; risk 32-34; self 11, 19, 31, 46, 83 (see also rhetoric); space 4, 13, 15-16, 18-20, 22-23, 25, 29, 45, 71, 73, 75-77; therapy 20; work disguised as 41 (see also Bergen, Doris)
play-based: approach 41; contexts xv, 36, 42, 47, 85; continuum 41; learning (PBL) 5-6, 35, 81
play cycle: adulteration 11-12, 18, 35, 51, 56-57, 62; annihilation 4, 6, 9-10, 12-14, 45-46, 48, 51-52, 56, 63, 77, 80; dysplay 30; flow xv, 4, 6, 9-14, 22, 37, 59, 77, 80, 85; loop and flow 9; meta-lude 9; play cue xiv-xv, 4, 6, 9-14, 16-17, 21-23, 28-31, 33, 35, 37-38, 41, 45-46, 48-63, 71, 75-78, 80, 83, 85; play return 4, 6, 9, 11-14, 16, 21, 28-29, 35, 37, 45-46, 48-56, 58, 61, 63, 77, 80, 83; play frame 4, 6, 9-14, 24, 35, 39, 45-46, 48, 51-54, 57, 62-63, 77, 80, 83; pre-cue xiv, 4, 6, 9-14, 16-17, 21, 23-24, 77, 80; witness position 31, 46
Play Cycle Observation Method (PCOM): analysis 6, 48-49, 52, 57-60, 63; application 6, 48-49; frequency and percentage table 60, 62, 87; record sheet 48-57, 60-63, 86-87; record sheet table 48-51, 54, 56-57, 60, 87; resources 6, 48
Play England 22
play maintenance 6, 11, 14, 18, 35-37, 39-43, 47, 56, 62, 76, 80 (see also Adult Intervention Style)
play policy: Play and Leisure Statement for Northern Ireland 65, 67; of Republic

of Ireland 65-66; Republic of Ireland, Teenspace 66; Scotland 65-66; Wales, play policy for 34, 65-66; Wales, Play Policy Implementation Plan 66

Play Scotland 66

play strategy: Northern Ireland, Play and Leisure Plan 67; Scotland, play strategy 66; Scotland, Play Strategy Action Plan 66; Wales, Play Policy Implementation Plan 66 (*see also* policy)

Play Sufficiency Assessment (PSA) (Wales) 66

play therapy (PT): directive 30; non-directive 30

play types: block 23; creative 23; communication 23; construction 23; deep 23; digital 18, 24; dramatic 23-24; exploratory 23; fantasy 23, 35; functional 18, 23; game design 18; games with rules 3, 24, 77 (*see also* Piaget, Jean; Whitebread, David); group 3, 36, 38; imaginative 18, 23; imitative 24; locomotor 23; Loose Parts Play (LLP) 21-22, 37 (*see also* Loose Parts); make-believe 24-25; mastery 23; musical 23; nature 18; object 3, 23-24, 77 (*see also* Whitebread, David); physical 3, 18-19, 24-25, 71, 77 (*see also* Whitebread, David); practice 24; pretend 3, 18, 22, 24-25, 77 (*see also* Piaget, Jean; Whitebread, David); recapitulative 23; risky 5, 18, 24-25, 33, 71 (*see also* play, Sandseter, Ellen B. H.); risky, dangerous elements 3, 24, 33; risky, dangerous tools 3, 24, 33; risky, getting lost 3, 24, 33; risky, great heights 3, 24, 33; risky, high speeds 3, 24, 33; risky, rough and tumble 3, 23-24, 33; role 23-24, 42; rough and tumble 3, 23-24, 32-33; sand 23; sensory 23, 25; social 3, 18, 23-24; social, associative 3, 24; social, co-operative 3, 24; social, onlooker 3, 24; social, parallel 3, 24; social, solitary 3, 24; social, unoccupied 3, 24; socio-dramatic (*see also* Smilansky) 23; socio-dramatic, imitative role play 24; socio-dramatic, interaction 24; socio-dramatic, make-believe 24; socio-dramatic, persistence 24; socio-dramatic, verbal communication 24; symbolic 3, 23-25, 77 (*see also* Piaget, Jean; Whitebread, David); taxonomy 3, 23 (*see also* Bob Hughes); transgressive 24

Play Wales 73

playful: elements 40; habit 8; interactions 20, 29; learning 41

PlayLink 3, 15

playgroups 5

playwork: approach 82; census 6; courses 71, 83; education and training 13; environments xv; healing, 1, 85; pathway 1; partnerships 1; pathway 1; playworkers 6, 9, 12-13, 22-23, 27-29, 31, 33, 37-40, 44, 46, 67, 84-85; practice 9-10, 27, 43, 73; principles 3, 9, 28, 83; principles in practice (P3) 73-74; principles, scrutiny group (PPSG) 3, 9, 28, 83 (*see also* playwork); profession 28; provision 43, 65, 68; qualifications 73-74; research 82 ; sector xiii; settings 68; team 2; theory xiii-xiv; trainer 71

Plowman, Lydia 24

Pollock, Irene 43

Power, Sally 27

practitioner: adult 11, 34, 39; childcare 65, 72, 80, 84; early years xv, 40, 72, 74, 78, 80, 84; play 81; playwork 36, 46, 65, 80, 84; reflective xiv, 6, 13, 35, 44, 46, 80; status 75, 78, 80; student 7, 14, 80

pre-school 5, 22, 42, 63

Prieske, Björn 18

Prison Advice Care Trust (PACT) 5

prisons 5, 85

professional practice 2, 6-7, 10, 12-13, 28, 40, 43, 45, 67, 72, 74, 76, 80-85

Profound and Multiple Learning Disabilities (PMLD) 29; *see also* atypicality

psycholudics 8

Public Services Reform (Scotland) Act 2010 69; *see also* legislation

Pyle, Angela 5-6, 35, 41, 47, 81

qualifications: childcare 8, 72, 83; customised 71; early years 8, 72; framework (Scotland) 73; higher education 75, 78, 80; playwork 8, 73, 83; professional 13, 82-83; staff 69; vocational 6, 14, 65, 68, 72-73, 83-84

Quennerstedt, Ann 26

Quaintrell, Yvonne 5

Rainham, Daniel 21

Rajan, Vinaya 27

Reed, Michael 43
reflection-in-action 43–47; *see also* Schön, Donald A.
reflection-on-action 43–47; *see also* Gibbs, Graham
reflective: practice 6, 13–14, 34–35, 43–48, 63, 73, 75, 77–78, 80; practitioner xiv
register: childcare 65, 68–70; early years 68–69; general childcare (compulsory) 69; general childcare (voluntary) 69; playwork 65, 68; provision 68; setting 71; *see also* Regulation and Inspection
Regulation and Inspection of Child Minding and Day Care (Wales) Order 2016 69; *see also* legislation
Rehman, Laurene 21
Rennie, Steve 30
Resources, Application, and Analysis (RAA) 6; *see also* Play Cycle Observation Method (PCOM)
Reynolds, Arthur J. 28
rhetoric 3, 83–84; *see also* Sutton-Smith, Brian
Rhys, Mirain 27
Ridgers, Nicola D. 19
risk: barriers to 34; benefit analysis 32–33; in play 6, 24, 26, 32–34, 76, 81, 83; taking 21
Roach, Lindsay 21
Robinson, Carol 26
Rohatyn-Martin, Natalia 21
Root, Amy E. 84
Rosengarten, Tricia 20
Ross, Gail 3, 40
Rothlein, Liz 84
Rubin, Kenneth H. 3, 63
Russell, Wendy 6, 11, 16, 35, 80
Ryan, Virginia 30

Salmi, Wedad N. 5
Sandberg, Anette 16, 19
Sando, Ole J. 18, 23, 25
Sandseter, Ellen B. H. 3, 18, 23, 25, 32–33
Sawyers, Janet K. 23
Sayers, Jo 19
Scheres, Anouk 25
Schneider, Barry H. 25, 30
Schön, Donald A. 43–45
schools 1, 4–5, 13, 15, 20–22, 25, 33, 41, 43, 66, 69, 72, 78, 84

Scott, Eric 32
Scott, Fiona 18, 24
Scottish Credit and Qualifications Framework (SCQF): Level 6 Childhood Practice 73–74; Level 6 The Social Services (Child and Young People) (Scotland) 74; Level 7 The Social Services (Children and Young People) including Modern Apprenticeships (Scotland) 74; *see also* qualifications, vocational
Scottish Qualifications Authority (SQA) *see* qualifications, vocational
Scottish Social Services Council (SSSC) 69
Scottish Vocational Qualifications (SVQ): Level 6 in Playwork 73; Level 7 in Playwork 73; Level 9 in Playwork 73; *see also* qualifications, vocational
Sector Skills Council (SSC) 72
senses *see* play, menu
Shamsudin, Iylia D. 29, 80, 81
Shloim, Netalie 90
Sidhu, Jeevita 23
simple involvement 6, 11, 14, 18, 35–37, 39, 41–43, 47, 52, 62, 76, 80; *see also* Adult Intervention Style
six elements (play cycle): Annihilation 4, 6, 9–10, 12–14, 45–46, 48, 51–52, 56, 63, 77, 80; definitions 9–10;
Flow 4, 6, 9–14, 22, 37, 59, 77, 80
Play cue 4, 6, 9–10, 12–14, 16–17, 21, 23, 28–30, 33, 35, 37–38, 45–46, 48–52, 54–57, 59, 61–63, 76–78, 80, 83
Play return 4, 6, 9, 11–14, 16, 21, 28–29, 35, 37, 45–46, 48–56, 58, 61, 63, 77, 80, 83
Play Frame 4, 6, 9–14, 24, 35, 39, 45–46, 48, 51–54, 57, 62–63, 77, 80, 83
Pre-cue xiv, 4, 6, 9–14, 16–17, 21, 23–24, 77, 80
Sleet, David A. 33
Slotkin, James S. 2–3
Smilansky, Sara 24
Smith, Joanne L. 18
Smith, Peter K. 3, 32, 83
Smith, Stephen 28
Smith-Gilman, Sheryl 20–21
Social Care Wales (SCW) 72, 74, 78
Soucisse, Marie M. 25
space: conceived 16; indoor 25; lived 16; natural 8; outdoor xv, 6, 17, 20–21; open 2, 5; perceived

16; physical 19, 51; play 4, 13, 15-16, 18-20, 22-23, 25, 29, 45, 71, 73, 75-77; potential 10; psychological 51; public 25; shared 29; therapeutic 1, 8
spatial triad 16; see also Lefebvre, Henri
Spiegal, Bernard 32, 34
Spencer, Rebecca 20
Standard Setting Organisations (SSO) 72; see also Sector Skills Council
statutory: curricula 41; duty 66; requirement 70
Stewart, Tracey 43
St. George, Jennifer M. 32
Stobart, Tanny 1
Stone, Michelle R. 20-21
Stordal, Gjertrud 18, 27
Storli, Rune 18-19
Sturrock, Gordon xiii-xiv, 1-2, 4, 6-11, 13, 15, 30-31, 35, 39, 41, 46, 80, 84-85; see also 'Colorado Paper'
Sutton-Smith, Brian 3, 83
Szafraniec, Grazyna 30

Take 10 for Play 1
Target Child (TC) 49-63, 87; see also Play Cycle Observation Method (PCOM)
Taylor, Chris 27
Taylor, Keirsten 21
Taylor, Meaghan E. 40
Taxonomy of Play Types 3, 23; see also Bob Hughes
teacher directed 41; see also play-based, learning
Temple, Susannah 31, 34, 46
The playground as therapeutic space: playwork as healing 'The Colorado Paper' xiii-xiv, 1, 7-9, 13, 84-85; see also 'Colorado Paper'
theory: cognitive development 3; ecological systems 81 (see also Bronfenbrenner, Urie); loose parts 10, 13, 15, 20; play 3, 28, 83; play cycle xiii-xiv, 1-2, 4, 6, 8, 10-11, 13-14, 40, 44, 73; playwork xiii-xiv
therapist 30-31; see also play therapy
third area 10; see also space, potential
Thomas, Gary 43
Toub, Tamara S. 27
Tsaloglidou, Areti 5
Turner, Joan 21
TULSA 70, 83; see also Regulation and Inspection

UK Commission for Employment and Skills 43, 72
umwelt 16-17; see also environment, functional cycle
United Nations (UN): Convention on the Rights of the Child (UNCRC) 6, 26, 65, 67, 80; CRC (Incorporation) (Scotland) Act 2024 67; International Children's Emergency Fund (UNICEF) 6, 26, 65, 80; Nations Convention of the Rights of the Child (Incorporation) (Scotland) Act 2024 (see also legislation)
Usher, Wendy 23

Vaisarova, Julie 28
variables 20-22; see also loose parts
verbal 9, 24, 28-29, 52, 57, 62, 76
Verma, Mohini 6, 24-25
Vickerius, Maria 16, 19
Vollstedt, Ralph 3, 83
von Uexküll, Jakob 10, 14-17, 25
Vygotsky, Lev 3, 22, 40; see also Zone of Proximal Development

Waldron, Sam 27
Warash, Barbara G. 84
Wardle, Francis 23
Wasteland 18; see also Kyttä, Marketta
Waters, Jane 28
watcher self 31
Webster, Alison 5
Weisberg, Deena S. 6
Wenger, Etienne 43
well-being 32, 66, 70, 77
Welsh Joint Education Committee (WJEC) 72, 74; see also qualifications, vocational
Whitebread, David 6, 23-25
Wilber, Ken 9
Willans, Becky 29
Wing, Lorna 29
Winnicott, Donald 9-10
Wisneski, Debora B. 84
Withagen, Rob 18
Witness Position 31, 46
Wood, David 3, 40
Wood, Elizabeth 27, 83
Woodall, James 5
Woods, Annie 28
Woolley, Helen 15

workers: childcare 2, 6-9, 12-13, 33, 40, 72, 84-85; early years 6-8, 12-13, 33, 40, 72, 84-85; education 8; nursery 85; playworkers 6-9, 12-14, 22-23, 33, 40, 84-85; school 85
Wraparound Care (WAC) 4-5, 72

Yamada-Rice, Dylan 18, 24

Zaal, Frank T. J. M. 18
Zachariou, Antonia 23
Zone of Proximal Development (ZPD) 3, 22, 40; *see also* Vygotsky, Lev

For Product Safety Concerns and Information please contact our EU representative  GPSR@taylorandfrancis.com
Taylor & Francis Verlag GmbH, Kaufingerstraße 24, 80331 München, Germany

DOI: 10.4324/9781003594819-1

DOI: 10.4324/9781003594819-5

## 38 The Play Cycle in practice

DOI: 10.4324/9781003594819-6

| Record Sheet | Play Cue Issued | | | Play Return | | | | Time | Play Cues in Established Play Cycles | | | |
|---|---|---|---|---|---|---|---|---|---|---|---|---|
| | Column 1 TC | Column 2 N-TC | Column 3 A | Column 4 TC | N-TC | A | N-H | Column 5 | Column 6 TC | Column 7 N-TC | Column 8 A |
| PCOM 1 | ✓ | | | | | ✓ | | 2 min 11 secs | | | |
| PCOM 2 | | ✓ | | ✓ | | | | 18 secs | | ✓ | |
| PCOM 3 | ✓ | | | | | | ✓ | 11 secs | | | |
| PCOM 4 | | | | | | | | | | | |
| PCOM 5 | | | | | | | | | | | |
| PCOM 6 | | | | | | | | | | | |
| PCOM 7 | | | | | | | | | | | |
| PCOM 8 | | | | | | | | | | | |
| PCOM 9 | | | | | | | | | | | |
| PCOM 10 | | | | | | | | | | | |
| PCOM 11 | | | | | | | | | | | |
| PCOM 12 | | | | | | | | | | | |
| PCOM 13 | | | | | | | | | | | |
| PCOM 14 | | | | | | | | | | | |
| PCOM 15 | | | | | | | | | | | |
| PCOM 16 | | | | | | | | | | | |
| PCOM 17 | | | | | | | | | | | |
| PCOM 18 | | | | | | | | | | | |
| PCOM 19 | | | | | | | | | | | |
| PCOM 20 | | | | | | | | | | | |
| Add Up Each Column | TC lay Cues | N-TC Play Cues | A Play Cues | Play Cycles Formed (Add All the Returns Together) | | | | Add All Times Together | TC Play Cues | N-TC Play Cues | A Play Cues |
| Total | 2 | 1 | 0 | 1 TC + 1 A + 1 N-H = 3 | | | | 2 minutes 40 seconds | 0 | 1 | 0 |
| Average | 67% | 33% | 0% | 100% | | | | | 0% | 100% | 0% |

84  *The Play Cycle in practice*

www.ingramcontent.com/pod-product-compliance
Lightning Source LLC
Chambersburg PA
CBHW062139160426
43191CB00014B/2333